POWER HUNGRY®

POWER HUNGRY®

THE ULTIMATE ENERGY BAR COOKBOOK

CAMILLA V. SAULSBURY

LAKE ISLE PRESS, INC., NEW YORK

Published by:
Lake Isle Press, Inc.
2095 Broadway, Suite 301
New York, NY 10023
(212) 273-0796
E-mail: info@lakeislepress.com

Distributed to the trade by:
National Book Network, Inc.
4501 Forbes Boulevard, Suite 200
Lanham, MD 20706
1(800) 462-6420
www.nbnbooks.com

Library of Congress Control Number: 2013941821

ISBN-13: 978-1-891105-54-8
ISBN-10: 1-891105-54-X

Book and cover design: Ellen Swandiak
Editor: Jennifer Sit

This book is available at special sales discounts for bulk purchases as premiums or special editions, including customized covers. For more information, contact the publisher at (212) 273-0796 or by e-mail: info@lakeislepress.com

First edition
Printed in the United States of America

10 9 8 7 6 5 4 3 2 1

FOR CAROL KERSH SIMONS

A teacher who inspired me for a lifetime and taught me
how to embrace creativity at every opportunity.

ACKNOWLEDGMENTS

My sincerest thanks and appreciation, and a batch of homemade energy bars anytime and anywhere, goes out to the following people.

To my savvy, talented, cheer-leading agent, Clare Pelino. If you hadn't taken the time to chat, out of the blue, on a cold, rainy afternoon in New York, this book would not have happened. Thank you for introducing me to Lake Isle Press; it is a perfect fit for this project, in every way. You are a superstar.

To Hiroko Kiiffner and Jennifer Sit: I knew I was in excellent hands from the moment we began our first conference call. I cannot say enough about your kindness, encouragement, creativity, generosity, and hard work in making this book a reality. I love that you included me on every detail of the book's process and encouraged me to push the possibilities for this book. Plus, you are both such delightful, considerate people. I consider myself very lucky indeed to be working with two such talented women!

Heaps of thanks and praise are also due to Ellen Swandiak, the brains behind the design of this book. I was a nervous wreck upon arriving at the first day of the food photoshoot; you swept it all away the moment I walked through the door and you instructed me to make myself at home (followed by an offer of a freshly brewed cup of coffee, which was exactly what I needed).

To Tina Rupp, photographer extraordinaire: I was a huge fan of your work before we met, and yet you still managed to surpass my expectations. What a thrill, too, to find out that the woman behind the photographs is every bit as phenomenal. I had so much fun working with you and could not be happier with the final images.

To Kevin and Nick, for all of your combined love and support, as well as for eating so many of my homemade energy bars over the years (even some of my less successful experiments/mistakes). You give me so much energy and inspiration—I love you with all my heart. Thank you, too, for (1) disappearing to the park for several hours when I needed some extra time to meet deadlines; and (2) understanding when I was too pooped from testing power bar recipes all day to make dinner.

To my parents, Dan and Charlotte, for supporting every one of my new ventures—always—with unwavering support and love.

Finally, to all of my fitness class participants, fitness buddies, and the readers of my blog, Power Hungry: your feedback of, and enthusiasm for DIY energy bars is what prompted me to keep creating new recipes and eventually sparked the idea for this project. This book is for all of you.

Here's to being power hungry!

TABLE OF CONTENTS

FOREWORD

This book has been more than a decade in the making. It all began in my twenties, the better part of which I spent eating out of my backpack.

My twenties meant graduate school, and that translated to working a ridiculous number of jobs, including, but not limited to, fitness instructor, sociology instructor, food columnist, and personal trainer. Oh, and then there was the business of being a graduate student and completing my Ph.D.

The logistics of planning and packing healthy meals and snacks to sustain me through my busy days was tricky. All told, I did my best to stuff assorted Tupperware and baggies full of cut-up vegetables, gorp, trail mix, dried fruit, granola, salads, whole grain sandwiches, and leftover tofu casserole.

But one can only carry so many pounds of food on one's back without eventually sliding into hobo-hood. Lucky for me, I recognized my need for a lightweight solution before it was too late. I soon found it in an all-too-convenient wrapper: power bars.

In retrospect, it was a deal with the devil: lighten the load, but lose the flavor. I stomached many a bar with the taste and texture of a peanut butter sponge, complemented by a soupçon of band-aids and a chocolate Ex-Lax-like coating. Power bars (my preferred term because it includes all varieties of nutrition bars such as energy bars, protein bars, and activity bars) have come a long way in recent years, but my dependence began in the late nineties, a time when manufacturers were still determining how to make them taste like food.

At some point I came to my senses and headed to the kitchen to make my own.

A power bar, I soon discovered, requires little time, effort, or expertise to prepare. Making them is not rocket science, and only requires a minimum of kitchen science: combine some high energy ingredients (for example, nuts, dried fruits, seeds, whole grains, all-natural protein powder), hold it all together with some edible "glue" (for example, nut or seed butter, honey, maple syrup, pumpkin purée, even mashed beans), pop into the oven for a few minutes—or, in many cases, simply press into a pan and chill—then cut into bars.

And the results? Delicious. All-natural. Endlessly versatile. Perfectly portable. And ever so frugal, to boot.

Now it's your turn to seize the power, and with this book in hand, it's quite literally within your grasp.

INTRODUCTION

When power bars first appeared on store shelves in the 1980s, they were marketed to a niche group of athletes and bodybuilders looking for specialized fuel promising delivery of a competitive edge. Fast forward 30 years and the power bar industry is experiencing exponential growth—in the billions—across multiple markets.

A primary explanation for the dramatic increase is simple: we have become a nation of snackers. In today's on-the-run society, almost 50% of all eating by adults occurs between meals. Power bars are a perfect pick for our new style of quick, portable snack-meals. No longer an obscure eating option for fitness pros, power bars are now marketed to, and regularly eaten by, consumers of all ages and activity levels: as a tasty meal to go, a quick and healthy snack, a pre- or post-workout booster, a weight loss aid (to stave off hunger), or as a general nutrition booster for any lifestyle, activity, time of day, or place. In sum, power bars now have a permanent place in the modern American diet.

A second, but equally persuasive explanation for the newfound popularity of power bars is the rapid growth in the numbers of Americans participating in fitness activities. Despite all of the news about overeating and obesity, more than 50 million Americans now belong to health clubs, a 10% increase over the past three years. Further, participation in athletic events—triathlons, marathons, 10Ks, mud-runs, and more—is at an all-time high. Power bars constitute ideal food for these fitness enthusiasts, easily packed in a pocket, pouch, or gym bag.

THE PROBLEM WITH STORE-BOUGHT ENERGY BARS

Despite the plethora of power bars on the market, something seemingly counterintuitive is occurring: people are opting to make power bars at home and scouring the internet to find recipes for doing so.

I have first-hand knowledge of the demand. When I first began publishing recipes for simple, homemade power bars on my healthy cooking blog several years back, I never dreamed that they would end up getting millions of hits. And mine is not an isolated occurrence: homemade power bars are enjoying the limelight in countless blogs, tweets, Pinterest boards, and all manner of food, health, and fitness websites.

Hence the conundrum: if daily life feels more time-crunched than ever, why on earth make homemade versions of a readily available convenience food?

While there are idiosyncratic reasons contributing to the trend, two key issues are driving it: cost and ingredient control. I would be happy to geek out at this point and illustrate my position with flow charts, graphs, and statistical analyses, but (thank heavens), this is one enigma that is easily explained.

1. COST

Power bars retail for anywhere between one and four dollars apiece, depending on the type of bar (for example, high protein bars cost far more than basic energy bars) and where it's purchased (for example, bars cost far less at warehouse club stores than at health food stores or gyms). While a single bar won't break the bank, the cost of eating multiple power bars in a week's time—typical for fitness enthusiasts and multi-person families—can quickly become prohibitive.

2. INGREDIENT CONTROL

I contend ingredient control is an even more compelling argument than cost. The demand for all-natural, high-quality food is fast becoming the rule rather than the exception and people of all stripes and sorts are seeking greater control over the food they eat, and that includes power bars. Ironically, a large percentage of power bars on the market are loaded with a range of unhealthy ingredients such as synthetic flavorings, artificial sweeteners, soy protein isolate, sugar alcohols, hydrogenated oils, chemical colorants, and high-fructose corn syrup. Additional ingredient control factors driving consumers towards DIY power bars include the following:

POOR TASTE: "Poor" taste is putting it nicely. A consistent complaint about ready-to-eat power bars is the flavor—they are too sweet, cloying, or have a peculiar taste from the protein ingredients. Further, despite hundreds of brands on the market, the same tastes and textures are employed again and again (think peanut butter and chocolate, double chocolate fudge, chocolate and peanut butter, double peanut butter chocolate, etc.), inevitably leading to power bar palate fatigue.

ARTIFICIAL PRESERVATIVES: The majority of power bars on the market—even many of the bars touting "natural" labels—contain synthetic, artificial preservatives to ensure a long shelf life and create a more visually appealing product. Part of the problem is that, while labels such as "organic" are federally regulated, wording such as "natural" and "all-natural" are not; manufacturers are able to define the terms as they choose. Homemade bars require no such artificial, ingredients, or potentially misleading advertising.

LOW-QUALITY PROTEIN: The protein in power bars is a large part of their appeal—it helps control appetite, build and repair muscle, maintain healthy bones, and much more—and is something that sets power bars apart from other portable snacks. However, the protein used in ready-made bars is typically very low-quality options, such as hydrolyzed animal collagen and hydrolyzed gelatin. Another low-quality protein that is used extensively, even in "all-natural" bars, is soy protein isolate, a waste product gleaned from the processing of primary soy products, such as tofu.

HIGH-ALLERGEN INGREDIENTS: An estimated 25 million Americans suffer from food allergies and several of the top food allergens—soy, gluten, corn, egg, dairy, and nuts—are principal ingredients in manufactured power bars. Even if the bars do not contain one or more of these ingredients, they are typically manufactured in plants that process such foods, which raises concerns of cross contamination and eliminates them as an option.

THE SOLUTION

But take heart, all-natural, affordable power bars are possible, and *Power Hungry* is delicious, nutritious proof.

Power Hungry has a simple premise: do-it-yourself power bar recipes that emphasize taste, maximize nutrition, minimize cost, and eliminate the junk can be made at home with ease and flair. The recipes cover a broad spectrum of fresh flavors and textures, including plenty of familiar flavor combinations, but also innovative twists and captivating new tastes. The result is more than 40 recipes with countless variations that empower you to hand-select superior ingredients, including the best complex carbohydrates—think rolled oats, multigrain cereals, and quinoa—and high-quality proteins—think nuts, seeds, dairy and nondairy milks, all-natural protein powders, and Greek yogurt.

There's even more to recommend these bars: making power bars from scratch affords control over food allergens, too. The overwhelming majority of recipes in this collection are easily made vegan and allergen-free with the suggested options. For example, swap seeds and seed butter for nuts and nut butter, gluten-free oats or quinoa flakes for regular oats, nondairy milk for dairy milk, and

vegan protein powder in place of whey protein powder. With *Power Hungry*, you create your bars, your way.

As promised, do-it-yourself power bars also grant far greater control of costs than ready-made bars. As a working mom, I keenly understand the management of grocery costs, so my focus throughout the book is for you to get the most bang for your buck. As such, I've tried my utmost to make sure that each and every recipe pays off multifold in taste, nutrition, affordability, and ease, and also offer a list of sources for buying ingredients in bulk and at discount prices.

I hope you encounter the same pleasure and health benefits I enjoyed while testing this collection of power bars. Some are based on recipes that I have been making for my family and myself for years. Others are new creations that draw inspiration from the expanding wealth of ingredients—for example, chia seeds, virgin coconut oil, quinoa—that have become widely available in supermarkets, as well as new dietary needs, styles, and philosophies (for example, gluten-free, raw, Paleo, and vegan) that have emerged. Each bar is unique, delicious, and a reminder that all-natural, homemade food needn't be complicated.

POWER HUNGRY PANTRY

While not an exhaustive list of every pantry item you might need, what follows is a guide to the fundamental ingredients I used to construct the recipes in this collection. These are everyday, any-day recipes, and the ingredients reflect that. The overwhelming majority of pantry items mentioned are readily available at well-stocked supermarkets. I use my small Texas town as a benchmark: if it is available here, then it is more than likely available where you live, too. A few less-than-usual ingredients make an appearance, too, but not without careful consideration. I have only included specialty ingredients that deliver a worthy bang for the buck, are versatile enough to be used in multiple recipes, and are extra-special in nutrition and taste. Still, if you choose not to buy these ingredients, I've designed the recipes in a way that allows for straightforward substitutions.

WHOLE GRAINS

ROLLED OATS Oats are a primary ingredient in many of the power bars in this collection, adding structure, flavor, and texture; they are to power bar-making what all-purpose flour is to baking.

Two types of rolled oats are called for in these recipes: large-flake (old-fashioned) rolled oats are oat groats (hulled and cleaned whole oats) that have been steamed and flattened with huge rollers; quick-cooking rolled oats are groats that have been cut into several pieces before being steamed and rolled into thinner flakes. For the best results, it is important to use the type of rolled oats specified in the recipe.

The overwhelming majority of the recipes in this collection are gluten-free, but many call for rolled oats. If you're following a gluten-free diet, be sure to to buy oats that are certified gluten-free. While ordinary rolled oats do not inherently have gluten, they can easily be contaminated with wheat during harvest, storage, or other stages of processing. Gluten-free oats are available in large-flake (old-fashioned) and quick-cooking varieties.

QUINOA Classified as a whole grain, but technically a seed, quinoa was a staple of the ancient Incas and is still an important food in South American cuisine. It contains more protein than any other grain and is considered a "complete protein" because it contains all eight essential amino acids. The tiny kernels cook like rice and expand to four times their original volume. The seeds are used toasted (crunchy) and cooked in water (chewy) in several power bar recipes throughout this collection; their flavor is earthy, with subtle nut and sesame-like flavors.

QUINOA FLAKES Quinoa flakes are made by steaming and flattening quinoa seeds with industrial-size rollers (just like the process to create rolled oats); they look like delicate, semi-translucent, quick-cooking oats. Quinoa flakes can be used as a measure-for-measure substitute for oats in any of the recipes; they will produce a lighter bar than oats.

AMARANTH Amaranth, like quinoa, is technically a seed, not a grain (specifically classified as a "pseudo-cereal"), and is a nutritional superstar. Though not a complete protein as quinoa is, it comes very close and what it does have to offer is pretty amazing: about three times the protein of most grains and high levels of iron, magnesium, phosphorus, and potassium. As if that weren't enough, it's also the only grain documented to contain vitamin C.

MILLET Millet is a tiny, mild-flavored grain that makes a crunchy, delicious addition to a wide range of bar recipes. Once toasted, it is a perfect alternative to nuts in any and all of the bar recipes in this collection.

NATURAL SWEETENERS

Natural sweeteners are closer to their whole form than refined sweeteners, which have most or all of their natural vitamins and minerals removed during the refining process. From a flavor perspective, natural sweeteners contain a broader spectrum of flavors than refined sugar; hence, they add more than sweetness alone to sweet and savory dishes.

DATES Dates—the fruit of the date palm tree—do double-duty in power bars. They contribute a rich flavor akin to dark brown sugar and, when processed in a food processor, can work as a multi-purpose binder. The most commonly available dates in the U.S. are Medjool dates, which are plump and tender, and Deglet Noor dates, which are semi-soft, slender, and a bit chewy; both work beautifully in these bars, so use what you can find. When choosing dates, select those that are plump-looking; it is okay if they are slightly wrinkled, but they shouldn't feel hard. See tip on page 20 for softening hard dates.

DRIED FRUIT Dried fruit is fundamental to homemade power bars, adding natural sweetness and, in many instances, acting as a "glue" to hold the bars together. Keep a variety of dried fruits at the ready for customizing

BEYOND OATS: OTHER ROLLED, 100% GRAIN FLAKES

While still relatively new to the market, several manufacturers have begun offering an assortment of other grain flakes—including spelt, kamut, rye, and brown rice—that are made in the same steaming and rolling process as rolled oats. Use any of these flake options as a measure-for-measure substitute for oats in any of the recipes in this book. Kamut or spelt power bars anyone?

TIP: SOFTENING DATES AND DRIED FRUIT IN WARM WATER

Not all dried fruits are created equally when it comes to moistness and softness. If what you have on hand resemble fossils more than fruits, give it a quick soak—from 2 to 10 minutes, depending on the toughness of the fruit—in warm (not hot) water. Drain the fruit and pat it dry between paper towels before using. Your teeth will thank you.

the flavors of your homemade bars in countless ways. Whenever possible, opt for organic dried fruit with no added sweeteners. The following are my top picks:

- Raisins (both dark and golden)
- Dried currants (sometimes labeled Zante currants)
- Dried cranberries (preferably sweetened with fruit juice, not sugar)
- Dried cherries
- Dried apricots
- Dried apples
- Dried figs
- Dried, unsweetened mangoes
- Dried, unsweetened pineapple
- Prunes (dried plums)

ORGANIC LIGHT CORN SYRUP Organic light corn syrup is an alternative to conventionally produced corn syrup. Conventional high fructose corn syrup is processed with chemicals and artificial additives and is used as a cheap sweetener in processed foods. By contrast, organic light corn syrup is made from GMO-free organic corn and is manufactured without chemicals, additives, or artificial flavors.

Corn syrup is specified in only a few recipes. It is a necessary ingredient for both recipes and other syrups, namely, honey, maple syrup, and agave nectar, will *not* work in its place. If you prefer to avoid corn syrup in these recipes, use an equal amount of my DIY Glucose Syrup (recipe page 30) in its place. If, however, you are comfortable using the organic corn syrup, feel free to substitute it—measure for measure—in any recipe calling for a syrup sweetener.

NATURAL (EVAPORATED) CANE SUGAR Evaporated cane sugar, also called whole cane sugar or dried cane juice, is made from the dried juice of the sugar cane plant. Many of the minerals from the plant are still present, which some studies suggest may help the human body digest the sugars. Dried cane sugar is less sweet than refined sugar and is available in a wide range of shades, from pale blonde to golden to deep brown; use the variety you prefer unless a recipe calls for a specific type. It can be substituted cup for cup for granulated sugar in baked goods. Trade names for this type of sugar are Rapadura and Sucanat.

HONEY Honey is plant nectar that has been gathered and concentrated by honey bees. Any variety of honey may be used in the power bar recipes in this collection. Unopened containers of honey may be stored at room temperature. After opening, store honey in the refrigerator to protect against mold. Honey will keep indefinitely when stored properly.

DIY GLUCOSE SYRUP (recipe page 30) Natural syrup can be pricey, so what's a frugal, power hungry person to do? Make your own organic cane glucose syrup, that's what! This syrup can be used for any of the recipes in this collection that call for honey, maple syrup, organic corn syrup, or agave nectar.

ARSENIC AND BROWN RICE SYRUP

Brown rice syrup is made from brown rice that has been soaked, sprouted, and cooked with an enzyme that breaks the starches into maltose. Until recently, it was used in many natural power bars. However, in 2012, researchers at the Dartmouth Children's Environmental Health and Disease Prevention Research Center found particularly high amounts of arsenic in brown rice syrup. Consumer Reports has raised concerns about arsenic levels in rice products in general, but it's the highly concentrated nature of brown rice syrup that is causing concern. Based on the available data, the FDA says consumers don't need to change their consumption of rice and rice products right now. Thus, you can always use an equal amount of my DIY Glucose Syrup (recipe page 30) in its place. I only suggest it as an alternative option for several bars that need the binding power of a glucose syrup. I encourage you to make your own decision—knowledge is power, and power is, after all, what this book is all about.

MAPLE SYRUP Maple syrup is a thick liquid sweetener made by boiling the sap from maple trees. It has a strong, pure maple flavor. Maple-flavored pancake syrup is just corn syrup with coloring and artificial maple flavoring added, and it is not recommended as a substitute for pure maple syrup. Unopened containers of maple syrup may be stored at room temperature. After opening, store maple syrup in the refrigerator to protect against mold. Maple syrup will keep indefinitely when stored properly.

AGAVE NECTAR Agave nectar (or agave syrup) is a plant-based sweetener derived from the agave cactus, native to Mexico. It has been used for centuries to make tequila, but it also adds a clean-tasting sweetness to power bars.

STEVIA Stevia is derived from the leaves of a South American shrub, *Stevia rebaudiana*. It is about 300 times sweeter than cane sugar, or sucrose. Stevia is not absorbed through the digestive tract, and therefore has no calories. Stevia comes in several forms: dried leaf, liquid extract, and powdered extract.

Liquid stevia is used in a small number of protein bars in this collection in order to keep carbohydrate levels at a minimum, but it can be also be used in any of the recipes—in combination with the specified sweetener—to add a subtle sweetness boost without added sugar and calories.

CHOCOLATE & COCOA

MINIATURE CHOCOLATE CHIPS Chocolate chips are small pieces of chocolate that are typically sold in a round, flat-bottomed teardrop shape. I like to use the miniature-size chips because a small amount can be easily dispersed throughout the bars. If regular chocolate chips are what you have handy, simply use the same amount as called for in the recipe, then chop into small pieces. Ideally, select chocolate chips that are all-natural and either grain-sweetened or sweetened with natural cane sugar. See the Ingredient Sources (page 142) for options, including

sources for vegan chocolate chips, gluten-free chocolate chips, all-natural white chocolate chips, and carob chips.

COCOA POWDER Select natural cocoa powder rather than Dutch process for the power bars in this collection. Natural cocoa powder has a deep, true chocolate flavor. The packaging should state whether it is Dutch process or not, but you can also tell the difference by sight: if it is dark to almost black, it is Dutch process; natural cocoa powder is much lighter and is typically brownish-red in color.

CACAO NIBS Cacao nibs are crumbled pieces of 100% cocoa beans and contain all of the antioxidant health benefits of the cocoa bean itself. The nibs are about the size of miniature chocolate chips and have a crunchy texture coupled with a nutty chocolate flavor. They have no added sugar, or any other added ingredients for that matter, making them a great choice for DIY power bars.

CANNED BEANS & DRIED LENTILS

Beans and lentils may sounds like odd additions to power bars, but in this case, odd equals awesome. Both are packed with nutrition, average 200 to 300 calories per cooked cup, and are low in fat and high in protein. In addition, they are inexpensive.

BEANS For the recipes that call for canned beans in this book, opt for varieties that are free of or low in sodium and have no added seasonings. If low- or no-sodium beans are unavailable, buy regular, unseasoned beans and rinse them thoroughly under cold water to remove as much sodium as possible.

LENTILS The recipes that call for lentils in this book require cooking, but it's a snap because lentils require no presoaking and cook from 20 to 45 minutes (depending on the type of lentil).

NUTS, SEEDS, & NUT/SEED BUTTERS

Nuts and seeds—including natural nut and seed butters—are very nutritious. In addition to being excellent sources of protein, nuts and seeds contain vitamins, minerals, fiber, and essential fatty acids (such as omega-3 and omega-6).

NUTS I use a wide variety of nuts in this collection, including walnuts, cashews, pecans, almonds, peanuts, hazelnuts, and pistachios. A number of the power bar recipes call for the nuts to be toasted before they are used. Toasting nuts deepens their flavor and makes them extra-crisp, two great qualities for any power bar. To toast whole nuts, spread the amount needed for the recipe on a rimmed baking sheet. Bake in a preheated 350°F oven for 8 to 10 minutes or until golden and fragrant. Alternatively, toast the nuts in a dry skillet over low heat, stirring constantly for 2 to 4 minutes or until golden and fragrant. Transfer the toasted nuts to a plate and let them cool before chopping.

GROUND FLAXSEEDS (FLAXSEED MEAL) Flaxseeds are highly nutritious, tiny seeds from the flax plant. They have gained tremendous popularity in recent years, thanks to their high levels of omega-3 fatty acids. But to reap the most benefits from the seeds, they must be ground into meal. Look for packages of ready-ground flaxseeds, which may be labeled "flaxseed meal," or use a spice or coffee grinder to grind whole flaxseeds to a very fine meal. The meal adds a warm, nutty flavor to a wide range of recipes. Flaxseeds are available in two basic varieties: brown or golden. They are equally fabulous and completely interchangeable so use what you can find or what you already have on hand. Flaxseeds—both whole and ground—can become rancid quickly due to their high oil content. To keep them fresh as long as possible, store them in an airtight container in the refrigerator for up to 5 months or in the freezer for up to 8 months.

GREEN PUMPKIN SEEDS (PEPITAS) Pepitas are pumpkin seeds with the white hull removed, leaving the flat, dark green inner seed. They are subtly sweet and nutty, with a slightly chewy texture when raw and a crisp, crunchy texture when toasted or roasted.

CHIA SEEDS Chia is an edible seed that comes from the desert plant *Salvia hispanica*, a member of the mint family that grows abundantly in southern Mexico. The seeds are very rich in omega-3 fatty acids (even more than flaxseeds) and are so rich in antioxidants that they don't deteriorate and can be stored for long periods without becoming rancid. Chia seeds also provide fiber (25 grams give you 6.9 grams of fiber) as well as calcium, phosphorus, magnesium, manganese, copper, iron, molybdenum, niacin, and zinc.

The seeds have a subtle, nutty flavor, and they do not need to be ground to make their nutrients available. You can substitute them for nuts and other seeds in almost any power bar recipe.

HEMP HEARTS (SHELLED HEMP SEEDS) Hemp hearts are the shelled, soft-textured seeds of hemp plants. They have a delicate flavor akin to pine nuts or walnuts and are nutrition powerhouses. They contain all 10 essential amino acids, are a rich and balanced source of omega-3 and omega-6 fatty acids, and are also rich in B vitamins, folic acid, phosphorus, potassium, magnesium, and calcium. They can be used in place of nuts—either raw or toasted—in any of the power bar recipes in this collection.

SHELLED SUNFLOWER SEEDS Sunflower seeds are highly nutritious and have a mild, nutty flavor and texture. The recipes in this collection call for seeds that have been removed from their shells. They can be used in place of nuts—either raw or toasted—in any of the power bar recipes in this collection.

SESAME SEEDS Tiny and delicate, the flavor of sesame seeds increases exponentially when they are toasted. They can be used to replace some of the nuts—either raw or toasted—in any of the power bar recipes in this collection.

NUT AND SEED BUTTERS Delicious, nutritious, ultra-convenient nut and seed butters are a boon for any meal of the day, as well as for snacks, desserts, and quick breads. They can also impart instant richness to a wide range of sauces and dressings.

All-natural, unsalted, unsweetened nut and seed butters are increasingly available at well-stocked supermarkets, co-ops, and natural food stores. Seed butters, such as tahini, sunflower seed butter, and hemp seed butter, are excellent substitutions for nut butters for those with tree nut allergies or sensitivities.

Below are some of the butters used in this collection. They may be used interchangeably in any recipe calling for nut or seed butter, unless otherwise specified. Very importantly, make sure to use smooth nut or seed butters throughout, not chunky. Store opened jars in the refrigerator.

- Unsweetened, natural peanut butter
- Unsweetened, natural almond butter
- Unsweetened, natural cashew butter
- Tahini (sesame seed butter)
- Unsweetened sunflower seed butter
- Unsweetened hemp seed butter

FATS & OILS

Fats and oils can be healthy or unhealthy; it all depends on the type you use and how much you consume. Here are my recommendations:

NONSTICK COOKING SPRAY Nonstick cooking spray is extremely helpful in shaping bars as well as preventing them from sticking to the pan. While any variety of cooking spray may be used, I recommend using an organic cooking spray for two reasons: first, these sprays are typically made with higher-quality oils (in many cases expeller-pressed or cold-pressed oils) than most commercial brands; second, they are more likely to use compressed gas to expel the propellant, so no hydrocarbons are released into the environment. Read the label and choose wisely.

VEGETABLE OIL "Vegetable oil" is a generic term used to describe any neutral, plant-based oil that is liquid at room temperature. You can choose any vegetable oils you prefer (for example, safflower, sunflower, canola), but for optimal health benefits, I suggest you opt for those that are:

1. Expeller-pressed or cold-pressed: expeller-pressed oils are pressed simply by crushing the seeds, while cold-pressed oils are expeller-pressed oils that are produced in a heat-controlled environment. Both types of oils avoid chemicals in their extraction process.

2. High in healthful unsaturated fats (no more than 7% saturated fat)

UNREFINED VIRGIN COCONUT OIL Virgin coconut oil can be used in both cooking and baking. It is semi-solid at room temperature and must be melted slowly, over low heat, to avoid burning. In some recipes, vegetable oil can be used in place of coconut oil, but in others, coconut oil helps to hold the bars together (it solidifies when cool), so consult the recipe tips before attempting a switch.

EGGS, DAIRY, & NONDAIRY MILKS

Eggs and dairy products are used sparingly in the power bar recipes in this collection. Nondairy milk can be used in place of dairy milk throughout the book, as indicated.

Using nondairy milk in place of dairy milk is a simple way to make many of the bars in this collection vegan, as well as accessible to those who are lactose intolerant or allergic to dairy. Although nondairy milks are available in a variety of flavors, opt for plain when substituting for milk in any of the recipes in this collection.

EGGS The power bar recipes in this book that call for eggs were tested with large eggs. Select clean, fresh eggs that have been handled properly and refrigerated. Do not use dirty, cracked, or leaking eggs, or eggs that have a bad odor or unnatural color when cracked open; they may have become contaminated with harmful bacteria, such as salmonella.

LOW-FAT MILK The power bar recipes in this book that call for dairy milk were tested with low-fat milk. However, equal amounts of skim (nonfat) milk or whole milk can be used in its place without compromising the bars, so use the dairy milk you have on hand. Alternatively, use one of the nondairy milk options listed below.

GREEK YOGURT Greek yogurt is a thick, creamy yogurt similar in texture to sour cream. It is made by straining the whey from yogurt and is very high in protein, not to mention incredibly delicious. I used nonfat, plain Greek yogurt for testing the recipes in this collection.

SOY MILK Soy milk is made by combining ground soybeans with water and cooking the mixture. The liquid is pressed from the solids and then filtered.

ALMOND MILK Almond milk is made from almonds, water, sea salt, and typically, a small amount of sweetener. It works particularly well as a substitute for dairy milk in baked good recipes.

RICE MILK Rice milk is made from brown rice, water, sea salt, and typically, a small amount of oil. It is a very light, sweet beverage that can replace cow's milk in most recipes.

HEMP MILK Hemp milk is a rich milk made from hemp seeds, water, and a touch of brown rice syrup. It is rich in healthy omega-3 fatty acids, protein, and essential vitamins and minerals. Because of its neutral taste, it can be used in a broad range of sweet and savory dishes.

LIGHT COCONUT MILK Typically available in cans, light coconut milk adds instant exotic flair to curries, soups, and sauces; it is also fantastic in desserts, such as ice cream, that usually rely on heavy dairy products. It is readily available and very affordable at supermarkets. The light varieties have 50% to 75% less fat than regular coconut milk, but retain all of the tropical flavor and much of the lush texture. Nevertheless, you are welcome to use an equal amount of full-fat coconut milk in its place.

ALL-NATURAL PROTEIN POWDERS

Food sources for protein are plentiful, but using all-natural protein powder is a quick and convenient way to give your homemade power bars, and your body, a boost of essential amino acids (for example, when carrying chicken breasts and tofu cutlets in your purse isn't an option).

Some of the power bars recipes (notably the protein bars) call for specific amounts of protein powder, but the wonderful thing about DIY power bars is that you can add one or two tablespoons of protein powder to any recipe by reducing the dry ingredients by an equal amount. I used both whey and vegan, raw protein powders, naturally sweetened and naturally flavored with vanilla or chocolate, throughout the collection; choose the variety that suits your needs and your taste. Finally, although many protein powders are gluten-free, check the label if you are following a gluten-free diet.

ALL-NATURAL, SWEETENED WHEY PROTEIN POWDER
Derived from milk, whey is considered the fastest-digesting "complete" protein, which means that it contains all the essential building blocks of muscle (amino acids), including high amounts of branched chain amino acids (BCAA). BCAAs become depleted after exercise and are needed for the maintenance of muscle tissue. That's why it is so often recommended to consume whey within minutes after your sweat session to quickly repair muscle damage. Opt for whey protein powders that are all-natural, free of sugar, gluten, artificial flavors, and artificial colors, and sweetened using all-natural stevia. In addition, look for a brand that uses whey that is derived from farm-raised, pasture-grazed, grass-fed cows that are not treated with the synthetic bovine growth hormone rBGH (see Ingredient Sources on page 142).

ALL-NATURAL, SWEETENED VEGAN PROTEIN POWDER
Vegan protein powders are made from a proprietary blend of plant proteins, which often includes pea protein, hemp protein, and rice protein. These varieties of protein powder are typically raw as well as vegan, but be sure to consult the label if your preference is for a raw powder. Look for blends that are allergen-free, soy-free, non-GMO, naturally flavored, and naturally sweetened with stevia. Naturally flavored and naturally sweetened pea protein may also be used, but for best results, do not use soy protein. The brands of vegan protein powders used for testing in this collection include Sun Warrior, Garden of Life, and Growing Naturals brands.

FLAVORINGS

Here are my top recommendations for flavoring that will elevate your power bars from ordinary to extraordinary:

VANILLA EXTRACT Vanilla extract adds a sweet, fragrant flavor to dishes, especially baked goods. It is produced by combining an extraction from dried vanilla beans with an alcohol and water mixture. It is then aged for several months.

ALMOND EXTRACT Almond extract is a flavoring manufactured by combining bitter almond oil with ethyl alcohol. It is used in much the same way as vanilla extract. Almond extract has a highly concentrated, intense flavor, so measure with care.

SPIRULINA POWDER Spirulina is a dark green powder made from blue-green algae. It contains a wealth of essential nutrients, including high levels of protein and high concentrations of many other important vitamins and minerals, including B complex vitamins, vitamin E, carotenoids, iodine, iron, manganese, zinc, and essential fatty acids such as gamma linolenic acid (which is only otherwise found in mother's milk). It has more betacarotene than carrots and is one of the few plant sources of vitamin B12, essential for healthy nerves and tissues. You can add several teaspoons of spirulina powder (more or less to taste) to any of the power bar recipes in the collection for an incredible nutrition boost.

INSTANT ESPRESSO POWDER Stronger than regular instant coffee powder, a small amount of instant espresso powder can add a dramatic coffee flavor to a range of power bars (it is particularly good for enhancing chocolate flavors). Look for it where coffee is shelved at the supermarket; if unavailable, use double the amount of instant coffee powder in its place.

FINE SEA SALT All of the recipes in this collection that call for salt were tested using fine-grain sea salt.

Conventional salt production uses chemicals, additives, and heat processing to achieve the end product commonly called table salt. By contrast, unrefined sea salt contains an abundance of naturally occurring trace minerals. But if you're in a pinch, you can certainly use an equal amount of conventional table salt in its place.

GROUND SPICES Spices can transform the most modest ingredients into magnificent bars. To preserve their flavors, they should be stored in light- and air-proof containers, away from direct sunlight and heat.

With ground spices, freshness is everything. To determine whether a ground spice or dried herb is fresh, open the container and sniff. A strong fragrance means it is still acceptable for use. Some of my favorite spices for flavoring power bars are:

• Cinnamon
• Cloves
• Nutmeg
• Ginger
• Cardamom
• Pumpkin pie spice
• Chinese five-spice powder
• Cayenne or chipotle chile powder

CITRUS ZEST Zest is the name for the colored outer layer of citrus peel. The oils in zest are intense in flavor. Use a zester, a Microplane-style grater, or the small holes of a box grater to grate zest. Avoid grating the white layer (pith) just below the zest; it is very bitter.

SPECIAL DIETS

If you follow a gluten-free, vegan, or Paleo diet, you're in luck: all of the recipes in this collection are gluten-free, most are naturally vegan, and several are Paleo-friendly. What follows are tips for making and choosing the right bars for your needs.

GLUTEN-FREE A growing number of people are choosing to eschew gluten—the elastic protein in such grains as wheat, rye, barley, and spelt—by choice rather than medical necessity. Proponents of a gluten-free lifestyle believe that a gluten-free diet, in addition to treating celiac disease, may improve gastro-intestinal conditions, aid weight loss, increase mental clarity, help children with certain forms of autism, and benefit the treatment of some autoimmune disorders.

While all of the recipes in this collection are gluten-free (or, in a few cases, have a gluten-free variation), it is important to use clearly labeled, gluten-free versions of the following ingredients:

- Oats
- Baking powder
- Chocolate
- Vanilla extract
- Almond extract
- Protein powder
- Multigrain hot cereal

VEGAN All but a small number of recipes in this collection are naturally vegan, meaning that they are free of all animal products such as eggs and dairy. Many vegans also avoid granulated sugar because it uses a bone-char bleaching process; natural cane and organic brown sugars, which are recommended in this collection, avoid this process. If following a vegan diet, do not use honey, as it is not vegan; use one of the other suggested sweeteners, such as agave nectar or maple syrup, instead. Also, use a nondairy milk option in place of dairy milk, as indicated, and take note of vegan variations in recipes that call for dairy products or eggs.

PALEO The Paleo Diet, also known as the Stone Age Diet or Caveman Diet, advocates following the dietary habits of our Paleolithic, cave-dwelling ancestors: specifically, consuming wild game, meat, eggs, and seafood, and vegetables, fruit, seeds, and nuts. Absent from the diet are foods that developed during the agricultural and industrial eras such as grains, dairy, legumes, refined sugars, and any other processed foods. Ready-made Paleo power bars are almost impossible to find, but I have several delicious options:

- Paleo Power Pucks (page 102)
- Lucy Bars (with the exception of variations including oats) (page 48)
- Lemony Spirulina Bars (page 132)
- Paleo Chocolate Hemp Bars (page 135)
- Raw Paleo Chocolate Bars (page 139)
- Sticky Sesame Bars with Raw Chocolate Drizzle (page 140)

DIY GLUCOSE SYRUP

This multipurpose syrup can be used in place of any other syrup, but it also has the chemical structure that is needed to bind particular bars, especially those lacking other binders; honey, agave nectar, and maple syrup will not work in its place (if you have ever had a pan of homemade energy bars or granola bars result in crumbles, you know what I mean). The only (natural) alternatives are organic corn syrup and brown rice syrup. You should note that you will need to buy one piece of special equipment before you boil your first batch: a candy thermometer. Did you just start to panic? Please don't! The candy thermometer simply clips to the pan and insures that your efforts turn out perfectly. They are inexpensive, too, and available at any kitchen supply store; I've even seen them at well-stocked grocery stores. After just one batch, you'll have more than paid for the expense of the thermometer with your savings. **MAKES ABOUT 2 CUPS**

1 cup water

2 2/3 cups organic, granulated, light-colored natural cane sugar (evaporated cane juice)

1/2 teaspoon cream of tartar or fresh lemon juice

1/8 teaspoon fine sea salt

1. Set a small dish of water and the pastry brush directly beside the stove.

2. Combine the water, sugar, cream of tartar, and salt in a medium, heavy-bottom saucepan and stir with the stainless steel or silicone spoon until blended. Clip the candy thermometer to the side of the pan and set the pan over high heat. Do not stir the sugar after this point.

3. As the sugar comes to a boil, dip the pastry brush in the dish of water and brush down the sides of the pan to dissolve any sugar crystals that could cause the syrup to re-crystallize.

4. Bring the mixture to a full boil; you will no longer need to brush the sides of the pan. Continue boiling until the syrup just barely reaches a temperature of 240°F (it is preferable to be a few degrees under than a few degrees over). Immediately turn off the heat, remove the candy thermometer, and carefully move the pan to a cool spot on the stove or a cooling rack. Allow the syrup to sit undisturbed until it has cooled completely, at least an hour.

5. Carefully pour the cooled syrup into jars, seal with the lids, and store in the cupboard.

TOOLS

CANDY THERMOMETER that can clip to the side of the pan

STAINLESS STEEL OR SILICONE SPOON (do not use a wooden spoon)

PASTRY BRUSH

CLEAN GLASS JARS WITH LIDS (recycled jars are fine)

TIPS

—To make the cooled syrup easier to pour, remove the metal lid from the jar and then place in a saucepan of simmering water to warm the syrup until pourable (about 5 to 6 minutes). Alternatively, microwave the opened jar of syrup on High in 30-second intervals until pourable.

—This recipe can be doubled.

STORAGE

ROOM TEMP: 3 months

BAR COATINGS

Just like the frosting on the cake, a slick, all-natural coating on your bars can add panache, appeal, and a punch of extra flavor. You can add any of these coatings to any bar in the collection.

NUT OR SEED BUTTER COATING

COMBINE 3 tablespoons natural, unsweetened nut or seed butter, 1 1/2 tablespoons virgin coconut oil (warmed until melted), and 3 to 4 drops of liquid stevia (more or less to taste) in a small bowl until blended.

SPREAD or drizzle over cooled, uncut bars. Alternatively, dunk the ends of cut bars and place on an unlined cookie sheet.

REFRIGERATE for 30 minutes until the coating has hardened.

MAKES enough to coat one 8- to 9-inch pan of bars (double the recipe for a 9 by 13-inch pan).

CHOCOLATE OR WHITE CHOCOLATE COATING

MELT 1/3 cup semisweet, bittersweet, or natural white chocolate chips in a microwave or double boiler according to the package directions.

WHISK in 2 teaspoons virgin coconut oil until blended

SPREAD or drizzle over cooled, uncut bars. Alternatively, dunk the ends of cut bars and place on an unlined cookie sheet.

REFRIGERATE for 30 minutes until the coating has hardened.

MAKES enough to coat one 8- to 9-inch pan of bars (double the recipe for a 9 by 13-inch pan).

GREEK YOGURT COATING

MELT 1/4 cup natural white chocolate chips in a microwave or double boiler according to the package directions.

WHISK in 1 tablespoon virgin coconut oil until blended, then whisk in 1 tablespoon plain, nonfat Greek yogurt, 1 teaspoon at a time, until blended and smooth.

SPREAD or drizzle over cooled, uncut bars. Alternatively, dunk the ends of cut bars and place on an unlined cookie sheet.

REFRIGERATE for 30 minutes until the coating has hardened.

MAKES enough to coat one 8- to 9-inch pan of bars (double the recipe for a 9 by 13-inch pan).

MEASURING INGREDIENTS

Accurate measurement is important for preparing power bars to ensure consistent results time and again. Here are my tips for precise measuring:

DRY INGREDIENTS When measuring a dry ingredient, such as flour, cocoa powder, sugar, spices, or salt, spoon it into the appropriate-size dry measuring cup or measuring spoon, heaping it up over the top. Slide a straight-edged utensil, such as a knife, across the top to level off the extra. Be careful not to shake or tap the cup or spoon to settle the ingredient, or you will have more than you need.

MOIST INGREDIENTS Moist ingredients, such as brown sugar, coconut, and dried fruit, must be firmly packed in a measuring cup or spoon to be measured accurately. Use a dry measuring cup for these ingredients. Fill the measuring cup to slightly overflowing, then pack down the ingredient firmly with the back of a spoon. Add more of the ingredient and pack down again until the cup is full and even with the top of the measure.

LIQUID INGREDIENTS Use a clear plastic or glass measuring cup or container with lines up the sides to measure liquid ingredients. Set the container on the counter and pour the liquid to the appropriate mark. Lower your head to read the measurement at eye level.

EQUIPMENT

The equipment required to prepare the power bars in this collection is minimal. Here's what I suggest you have:

PANS
- 8-inch square metal, glass, or ceramic baking pan
- 9-inch square metal, glass, or ceramic baking pan
- 9 by 13-inch metal, glass, or ceramic baking pan
- 9 by 5-inch metal, glass, or ceramic loaf pan
- 12-cup muffin pan
- Large, rimmed baking sheet

APPLIANCES
- Food processor (medium to large size)
- Blender

KITCHEN TOOLS
- Large and medium mixing bowls
- 1-cup and 2-cup liquid measuring cups (preferably clear glass or plastic)
- Dry measuring cups in graduated sizes: 1/4 cup, 1/3 cup, 1/2 cup, and 1 cup
- Measuring spoons in graduated sizes
- Wire whisk
- Kitchen/chef's knife
- Cutting boards
- Wooden spoons
- Silicone or rubber spatulas
- Kitchen timer
- Box grater/shredder
- Oven mitts or holders
- Zester or Microplane-style grater
- Parchment paper
- Wire cooling rack
- Icing spatula (narrow-blade metal spatula for smoothly spreading bar coatings on finished bars)
- Candy thermometer (for DIY Glucose Syrup, page 30)

SUPER
NATURAL
KNOCK
OFFS

You know what your favorite ready-made bars are, and now you can make them (better!) at home. Re-create your favorite flavors or, better yet, experiment to create your own unique blend. Customizing bars is a convenient and frugal way to use up the odds and ends in the pantry, too. For example, if a recipe calls for 1/4 cup seeds or nuts, combine a tablespoon each of chia seeds, sunflower seeds, chopped peanuts, and chopped almonds; the same holds true for dried fruits. No matter which recipes, blends, or ingredients you settle upon, these super-natural knock-offs are sure to knock your socks off.

NICK BARS

(COMPARE TO *CLIF® BARS*)

1 cup packed pitted, soft dates

1 cup warm water

1 1/4 cups crisp brown rice cereal

1 cup quick-cooking rolled oats

1/4 cup coarsely chopped roasted or toasted nuts or seeds (e.g., peanuts, almonds, sunflower seeds)

2 tablespoons flaxseed meal

1/2 teaspoon ground cinnamon

1/2 cup natural, unsweetened nut or seed butter (e.g., peanut, cashew, or sunflower)

1/3 cup honey, agave nectar, or pure maple syrup

1 teaspoon vanilla extract

1/8 teaspoon fine sea salt

1/4 cup miniature semisweet chocolate chips

These were among the first homemade bars I ever tackled, and they remain one of my favorites many years later. The fact that they are free of soy protein isolate—an industrial waste product of the food processing industry—will make you jump (higher and stronger) for joy! **MAKES 12 BARS**

1. Line a 9-inch square baking pan with foil or parchment paper and spray with nonstick cooking spray.

2. Combine the dates and warm water in a small bowl. Let stand for 5 to 10 minutes until the dates are soft (time will vary according to the dryness of the dates). Drain and pat dry with paper towels.

3. Stir together the cereal, oats, nuts or seeds, flaxseed meal, and cinnamon in a large bowl.

4. Place the dates in a food processor. Using on/off pulses, process until finely chopped. Add to the bowl with the cereal.

5. In a small saucepan, combine the nut or seed butter and honey. Heat over medium-low, stirring, for 2 to 4 minutes until the mixture is melted and bubbly. Remove from heat and stir in the vanilla and salt.

6. Immediately pour the honey mixture over the cereal mixture, mixing with a spatula until coated. Gently stir in the chocolate chips.

7. Transfer the mixture to the prepared pan. Place a large piece of parchment paper, wax paper, or plastic wrap (coated with nonstick cooking spray) atop the bar mixture and use it to spread, flatten, and very firmly compact the mixture evenly in the pan. Cool at least 1 hour until firmly set.

8. Using the liner, lift the mixture from the pan and transfer to a cutting board. Cut into 12 bars.

BAR TIPS

—For a higher protein bar, reduce the rice cereal to 1 cup, omit the ground flaxseeds, and add 1/3 cup all-natural, sweetened vanilla or chocolate vegan or whey protein powder.

—You can use an equal amount of other puffed or crisp grain cereals, such as puffed millet, quinoa, or amaranth, in place of the crisp rice cereal.

BAR KEEPING

Tightly wrap the bars individually in plastic wrap.

ROOM TEMP: 3 days
REFRIGERATOR: 2 weeks
FREEZER: 3 months in airtight container; thaw 1 hour

Nutrients per bar: Calories 195, Fat 7.5 g, (Saturated 1.8 g), Cholesterol 1 mg, Sodium 41 mg, Carbs 29.8 g (Fiber 3.2 g, Sugars 19.8 g), Protein 4.9 g

BAR VARIATIONS

CRUNCHY PEANUT BUTTER BARS
Prepare as directed, but omit the chocolate chips and cinnamon. Use peanut butter and chopped, roasted, lightly salted peanuts for the nut butter and nuts.

CHOCOLATE ALMOND FUDGE BARS
Omit the cinnamon. Replace the flaxseed meal with 3 tablespoons natural, unsweetened cocoa powder (not Dutch process). Replace the vanilla with 3/4 teaspoon almond extract, and use almond butter and chopped toasted almonds for the nut butter and nuts.

OATMEAL RAISIN PECAN BARS
Replace the chocolate chips with 1/3 cup raisins, increase the cinnamon to 3/4 teaspoon, and use chopped toasted pecans for the nuts.

FRENCH DRIED PLUM BARS
Replace the dates with an equal amount of pitted moist prunes; skip the soaking in warm water. Replace the cinnamon with an equal amount of ground cardamom, use 1/2 cup walnuts for the nuts, and omit the chocolate chips.

BLUEBERRY, CHERRY, OR APRICOT ALMOND BARS
Replace the chocolate chips with 1/3 cup dried blueberries, dried cherries, or chopped dried apricots. Replace the vanilla with 3/4 teaspoon almond extract, and use almond butter and chopped toasted almonds for the nut butter and nuts.

CHOCOLATE BROWNIE BARS
Omit the cinnamon. Replace the flaxseed meal with 3 tablespoons natural, unsweetened cocoa powder (not Dutch process).

BANANA NUT BREAD BARS
Replace the chocolate chips with 1/4 cup finely crushed banana chips, add 1/4 teaspoon ground nutmeg, and use chopped toasted walnuts or pecans for the nuts.

GINGERBREAD BARS
Increase the cinnamon to 3/4 teaspoon and add 1 1/2 teaspoons ground ginger, 1/4 teaspoon ground nutmeg, and 1/8 teaspoon ground cloves. Omit the chocolate chips. Consider topping with White Chocolate or Greek Yogurt Bar Coating (see page 31).

FRIEND BARS (COMPARE TO *KIND*® BARS)

1 1/2 cups chopped assorted raw or toasted nuts and/or seeds (e.g., cashews, sunflower seeds, green pumpkin seeds, peanuts, pecans)

1/3 cup crisp brown rice cereal

1/2 cup chopped dried fruit (e.g., raisins, apricots, berries, dates)

1/3 cup DIY Glucose Syrup (see page 30), organic light corn syrup, or brown rice syrup

1/8 teaspoon fine sea salt (optional)

Middle Eastern and European sweets made from nuts, seeds, dried fruits, and a sweet syrup binding—such as gozinaki in Georgia and pasteli in Greece—have been around for centuries. Here, the essential idea finds new life as an uncomplicated, nourishing energy bar. Before you start making plans to substitute your favorite brand of agave nectar, honey, or maple syrup for the specified syrups, hear me out: it will not work. Instead of a stack of bars, you will have a pile of crumbles. I could go into a lengthy chemical discussion about the structure and properties of various sugars, but I won't (which will simultaneously disappoint my retired-chemist father, but please my editor). Just trust me on this one and I know you will be thrilled with your results. MAKES 10 BARS

1. Line an 8-inch square baking pan with foil or parchment paper and spray with nonstick cooking spray.

2. Preheat oven to 325°F.

3. Stir together the nuts or seeds, cereal, and dried fruit in a large bowl.

4. Add the syrup and salt (if using) to the nut mixture and stir until evenly coated.

5. Transfer the mixture to the prepared pan. Place a large piece of parchment paper, wax paper, or plastic wrap (coated with nonstick cooking spray) atop the bar mixture and use it to spread, flatten, and very firmly compact the mixture evenly in the pan. Discard the paper or plastic.

6. Bake in the preheated oven for 17 to 20 minutes or until slightly browned at the edges, but still somewhat soft at the center. Let cool 20 minutes in pan on a wire rack.

7. Using the liner, lift the mixture from the pan and transfer to a cutting board. Cut into 10 bars. Cool completely.

BAR TIP

—You can use an equal amount of other puffed or crisp grain cereals, such as puffed millet, quinoa, or amaranth, in place of the crisp rice cereal.

BAR KEEPING

Tightly wrap the bars individually in plastic wrap.

ROOM TEMP: 3 days
REFRIGERATOR: 2 weeks
FREEZER: 3 months in airtight container; thaw 1 hour

Nutrients per bar: Calories 150, Fat 8.6 g, (Saturated 0.5 g), Cholesterol 0 mg, Sodium 42 mg, Carbs 17.6 g (Fiber 1.3 g, Sugars 13.9 g), Protein 3.8 g

BAR VARIATIONS

APPLE PECAN BARS
Use chopped dried apples for the fruit, pecans for the nuts, and add 3/4 teaspoon ground cinnamon along with the syrup.

VERY NUTTY FRIEND BARS
Omit the dried fruit and increase the total amount of nuts to 2 cups.

SEEDS OF FRIENDSHIP BARS
Omit the dried fruit and use 2 cups raw or toasted seeds (e.g., pepitas, sunflower seeds, hemp seeds, sesame seeds) in place of the nuts.

ALMOND APRICOT BARS
Use chopped dried apricots for the fruit, 1 1/4 cups almonds for the nuts, and add 1/4 cup unsweetened flake or shredded coconut. Add 2 teaspoons finely grated orange zest or lemon zest along with the syrup.

COCONUT ALMOND BARS
Use unsweetened flake or shredded coconut for the fruit and almonds for the nuts. Add 3/4 teaspoon almond extract along with the syrup.

GINGER SESAME BARS
Use 1 cup almonds or cashews and 1/3 cup sesame seeds for the nuts and seeds and chopped dates for the fruit. Add 1 teaspoon ground ginger along with the syrup.

FITNESS FIBER BARS

(COMPARE TO *FIBER ONE® BARS*)

1 1/2 cups quick-cooking rolled oats

1 cup All-Bran®-style cereal, coarsely crumbled

1/2 cup crisp brown rice cereal

1/4 cup dried fruit, chopped (e.g., raisins, cherries, apricots)

1/4 cup toasted pecans or walnuts, finely chopped

1/3 cup flaxseed meal

1/2 cup DIY Glucose Syrup (see page 30), organic light corn syrup, or brown rice syrup

1/4 cup natural, unsweetened nut or seed butter (e.g., peanut, cashew, or sunflower)

1 1/2 teaspoons vanilla extract

1/4 teaspoon fine sea salt

Eat more fiber! You've probably heard the edict a million time before, but it's not exactly the most appealing culinary call to action—unless you're really jazzed about all things bran. But all bran banter aside, fiber is pretty great stuff. Yes, it keeps you regular, but it also helps you feel satisfied, maintain a healthy weight, and lower your risk of diabetes and heart disease. It can also be delicious, as these fiber-packed bars prove. MAKES 12 BARS

1. Line an 8-inch square baking pan with foil or parchment paper and spray with nonstick cooking spray.

2. Preheat oven to 325°F.

3. Stir together the oats, bran cereal, rice cereal, dried fruit, pecans, and flaxseed meal in a large bowl.

4. In a small saucepan, combine the syrup and nut or seed butter. Heat over medium-low, stirring, for 1 to 2 minutes until mixture is just melted. Remove from heat and stir in vanilla and salt.

5. Immediately pour the syrup mixture over the oats mixture, mixing with a spatula until coated.

6. Transfer the mixture to the prepared pan. Place a large piece of parchment paper, wax paper, or plastic wrap (coated with nonstick cooking spray) atop the bar mixture and use it to spread, flatten, and very firmly compact the mixture evenly in the pan. Discard the paper or plastic.

7. Bake in the preheated oven for 18 to 22 minutes or until golden at the edges, but still slightly soft at the center. Immediately press down the bars with the back of a spatula to further compact the bars. Let cool completely in pan on a wire rack.

8. Using the liner, lift the mixture from the pan and transfer to a cutting board. Cut into 12 bars.

Nutrients per bar: Calories 165, Fat 6.4 g, (Saturated 0.9 g), Cholesterol 0 mg, Sodium 100 mg, Carbs 25.5 g (Fiber 4.5 g, Sugars 14.9 g), Protein 4.7 g

BAR TIPS

—Old-fashioned oats may be used in place of the quick-cooking oats, but the latter are preferable. Because of their smaller size, they help to "glue" the bar together and create a more compact bar.

—You can use an equal amount of other puffed or crisp grain cereals, such as puffed millet, quinoa, or amaranth, in place of the crisp rice cereal.

—You can use an equal amount of other whole grain flakes, such as kamut, spelt, quinoa, or rice, in place of the oats.

—For a higher protein bar, omit the flaxseed meal and add 1/3 cup all-natural, sweetened vanilla or chocolate whey protein powder.

BAR KEEPING

Tightly wrap the bars individually in plastic wrap.

ROOM TEMP: 3 days
REFRIGERATOR: 2 weeks
FREEZER: 3 months in airtight container; thaw 1 hour

BAR VARIATIONS

CHEWY CHOCOLATE BARS
Decrease the total amount of flaxseed meal to 1/4 cup. Add 2 tablespoons natural, unsweetened cocoa powder (not Dutch process) along with the vanilla. Replace the dried fruit with 1/4 cup miniature semisweet chocolate chips.

CHEWY CHOCOLATE CHIP BARS
Replace the dried fruit with 1/4 cup miniature semisweet chocolate chips.

SALTY SWEET PRETZEL BARS
Replace the crisp brown rice cereal with an equal amount of crushed (not too fine) pretzels. Use dates for the dried fruit.

CHEWY COCONUT-ALMOND BARS
Replace the dried fruit with an equal amount of unsweetened flake or shredded coconut, replace the flaxseed meal with an equal amount of finely chopped toasted almonds, and replace the vanilla with 3/4 teaspoon almond extract.

LEMON-BERRY WONDERFUL BARS
Use dried cranberries or blueberries (or a combination) for the dried fruit and replace the vanilla with 2 teaspoons finely grated lemon zest.

POWER GRAB PROTEIN BARS

(COMPARE TO *POWERBAR PROTEINPLUS® BARS, PROMAX® BARS,* OR *PURE PROTEIN® BARS*)

1 cup old-fashioned or quick-cooking rolled oats

1 1/3 cups plain nondairy milk or low-fat milk

1/2 cup natural, unsweetened nut or seed butter (e.g., peanut, cashew, or sunflower)

2 teaspoons vanilla extract

1 1/3 cups lightly packed all-natural, sweetened vanilla vegan protein powder

High-protein bars can come with particularly staggering price tags, at times as high as four dollars per bar. Equally staggering is the ingredient list on many of the bars: hydrolyzed gelatin, glycerin, soy protein isolate, high fructose corn syrup, fractionated palm kernel oil, and artificial sweeteners, flavors, colors, and preservatives. The great news is that a basic, junk-free, high-protein bar is ridiculously easy to make, and at a fraction of the price, too; here it is. The bars have a fudge-like texture that can be customized with a slick of chocolate, spices, natural extracts, nuts and fruits, or a few chocolate chips. MAKES 8 BARS

1. Line an 8-inch square baking pan with foil or parchment paper and spray with nonstick cooking spray.

2. Place the oats in a food processor and process into a fine powder.

3. Add the milk, nut or seed butter, and vanilla to the processor bowl. Process, using on/off pulses, until the mixture is blended and smooth, stopping to scrape the sides and bottom of the bowl once or twice with a rubber spatula.

4. Add the protein powder to bowl; process using on/off pulses until all of the protein powder is incorporated, stopping to scrape the sides and bottom of the bowl once or twice with a rubber spatula.

5. Transfer the mixture to the prepared pan. Place a large piece of parchment paper, wax paper, or plastic wrap (coated with nonstick cooking spray) atop the bar mixture and use it to spread and flatten the mixture evenly in the pan. Cover and refrigerate overnight until very firm.

6. Using the liner, lift the mixture from the pan and transfer to a cutting board. Uncover and cut into 8 bars. Store in the refrigerator or freezer.

Nutrients per bar: Calories 223, Fat 10.5 g, (Saturated 2.3 g), Cholesterol 32 mg, Sodium 11 mg, Carbs 12.8 g (Fiber 2.2 g, Sugars 3 g), Protein 20.1 g

BAR TIPS

—Consider topping the bars with the Chocolate Bar Coating or Greek Yogurt Bar Coating (see page 31).

—Whey protein will not work in this recipe as written; the bars will have a gooey, sticky texture that will not hold together in bar form. But the problem is easily solved: simply increase the total amount of oats to 2 cups and reduce the amount of milk to 1/2 cup.

—You can form the mixture into any size or shape that suits your fancy, from balls to rounds to free-form mini bars.

BAR KEEPING

Tightly wrap the bars individually in plastic wrap.

REFRIGERATOR: 2 weeks
FREEZER: 3 months in airtight container; thaw 1 hour

BAR VARIATIONS

CHOCOLATE FUDGE BROWNIE PROTEIN BARS
Reduce oats to 3/4 cup. Replace the vanilla protein powder with an equal amount of all-natural sweetened chocolate vegan protein powder and add 1/4 cup unsweetened cocoa powder (not Dutch process).

CHOCOLATE CHIP COOKIE DOUGH BARS
Add 1/3 cup miniature semisweet or bittersweet chocolate chips, or cacao nibs, along with the protein powder.

CINNAMON ROLL PROTEIN BARS
Add 1 1/2 teaspoons ground cinnamon along with the vanilla. Consider topping with White Chocolate Bar Coating (see page 31).

CRANBERRY ORANGE BARS
Add 1/3 cup dried cranberries. Omit the vanilla and add 2 teaspoons finely grated orange zest.

MOCHA-MOTION BARS
Reduce oats by 2 tablespoons. Replace the vanilla protein powder with an equal amount of all-natural sweetened chocolate vegan protein powder (not soy). Add 2 tablespoons unsweetened cocoa powder (not Dutch process) and 1 tablespoon instant espresso powder along with the vanilla.

OATMEAL RAISIN BARS
Add 1/3 cup raisins and 1 teaspoon ground cinnamon or pumpkin pie spice.

LEMON PIE BARS
Use cashew, almond, or sunflower butter for the nut or seed butter. Reduce the milk to 1 1/4 cups and add 1 1/2 tablespoons lemon juice. Omit the vanilla and add 1 tablespoon finely grated lemon zest. Consider topping with White Chocolate Bar Coating or Greek Yogurt Bar Coating (see page 31).

CANYON CRUNCH
GRANOLA BARS
(COMPARE TO *NATURE VALLEY*® *CRUNCHY GRANOLA BARS*)

3 cups old-fashioned or quick-cooking rolled oats

1 1/4 cup crisp brown rice cereal

1/2 cup packed organic dark brown sugar

1/3 cup honey

3 tablespoons water

1/4 cup vegetable oil or virgin coconut oil

1/2 teaspoon fine sea salt

1 teaspoon ground cinnamon

1 teaspoon vanilla extract

For those who can't be bothered with fussy ingredients, this recipe is expressly for you. The oats mixture gets tamped down hard—I mean it, hard!—both before and after baking to ensure a crispy, crunchy substantial bar that can travel, and take you traveling, for many miles. **MAKES 16 BARS**

1. Line a 9 by 13-inch baking pan with foil or parchment paper and spray with nonstick cooking spray.

2. Preheat oven to 350°F.

3. Spread the oats on a large rimmed baking sheet. Bake in preheated oven for 10 to 12 minutes, shaking halfway through, until golden and fragrant. Transfer to a large bowl; stir in the cereal. Reduce oven temperature to 325°F.

4. Meanwhile, combine the brown sugar, honey, water, oil, and salt in a small saucepan. Heat over medium-low, stirring, for 5 to 6 minutes until the sugar is dissolved and the mixture is bubbly. Remove from the heat and stir in the cinnamon and vanilla.

5. Immediately pour the syrup mixture over the oats mixture, mixing with a spatula until coated.

6. Transfer the mixture to the prepared pan. Place a large piece of parchment paper, wax paper, or plastic wrap (coated with nonstick cooking spray) atop the bar mixture and use it to spread, flatten, and very firmly compact the mixture evenly in the pan. Discard the paper or plastic.

7. Bake in the preheated oven for 22 to 25 minutes or until deep golden brown. Immediately press down the mixture with the back of a spatula to further compact the bars. Let cool completely in the pan on a wire rack.

8. Using the liner, lift the mixture from the pan and transfer to a cutting board. Cut into 16 bars.

Nutrients per bar: Calories 134, Fat 4.5 g, (Saturated 0.6 g), Cholesterol 0 mg, Sodium 98 mg, Carbs 22.5 g (Fiber 1.5 g, Sugars 10 g), Protein 2.8 g

BAR TIP

—Please don't reduce or eliminate the honey and brown sugar in this recipe! The specific ratio of sugar and honey binds the ingredients; without it, you risk making granola, not granola bars.

BAR KEEPING

Tightly wrap the bars individually in plastic wrap.

ROOM TEMP: 5 days
REFRIGERATOR: 2 weeks
FREEZER: 3 months in airtight container; thaw 1/2 hour

BAR VARIATIONS

CINNAMON PECAN GRANOLA BARS
Increase the ground cinnamon to 2 teaspoons and add 1/3 cup chopped pecans to the bowl of oats.

MAPLE BROWN SUGAR GRANOLA BARS
Replace the honey with an equal amount of pure maple syrup and replace the vanilla extract with an equal amount of pure maple extract.

ALMOND LOVERS GRANOLA BARS
Omit the cinnamon. Add 1/2 cup finely chopped almonds to the bowl of oats and replace the vanilla with 1 1/4 teaspoons almond extract.

COCONUT CRUNCH BARS
Replace the cinnamon with an equal amount of ground ginger. Reduce the oats to 3 1/4 cups and add 1/2 cup unsweetened flake or shredded coconut.

FRUIT ENDURANCE
GEL BLOCKS
(COMPARE TO *CLIF SHOT BLOKS® ENERGY CHEWS*)

1 cup light-colored natural cane sugar or granulated sugar

1 cup organic 100% fruit juice or fruit nectar, pulp-free (e.g., apple, cherry, mango, or berry)

1 3-ounce pouch liquid fruit pectin

1/4 cup honey, agave nectar, or DIY Glucose Syrup (see page 30)

1/4 teaspoon fine sea salt

2 teaspoons fresh lemon juice

Call them electrolyte gels, endurance gels, sports gels, nutritional gels, carbohydrate gels, or "Mommy's homemade yummy gummies" (thanks, Nick!)—whatever the eponym, these pop-able fruit gels provide quick carbohydrates for exercise endurance and recovery. While gel blocks are commonly used in endurance sports, they are a great mini pick-up for any kind of fitness endeavor. When I bothered to look at the ingredients on the label one day (while recovering from price shock), I knew I could recreate them (I can be cocky that way). And so I did! The blocks remain gelled at room temperature, and since they rely on natural fruit pectin, not gelatin, they are 100% vegan, too. You can find the fruit pectin in supermarkets or hardware stores where canning products are shelved. **MAKES 45 SQUARES**

1. Lightly spray a 9 by 5-inch loaf pan with nonstick cooking spray.

2. In a medium saucepan, whisk the sugar, fruit juice, pectin, honey, and salt until thoroughly blended.

3. Bring mixture to a full boil over medium-high heat, whisking continuously. Reduce heat to medium and continue whisking for 5 minutes longer. Remove from heat and whisk in the lemon juice. Pour into the prepared pan.

4. Loosely cover the pan with a clean dish towel and let stand at least 12 hours until firm (do not refrigerate).

5. Invert the pan on a cutting board to release the gel. Using a sharp knife, cut into 1-inch squares.

BAR TIP

—Be sure to whisk constantly while boiling the fruit juice-pectin mixture or the pectin may form clumps.

BAR KEEPING

Store the gels in an airtight container in a cool area for up to 1 week. For longer storage, store in the refrigerator for up to 1 month. They will remain gelled at room temperature so simply wrap in plastic wrap or place in a small zipper-top plastic bag when heading out for an adventure.

Nutrients per serving (5 squares): Calories 130, Fat 0 g, (Saturated 0 g), Cholesterol 0 mg, Sodium 67 mg, Carbs 33.7 g (Fiber 0.5 g, Sugars 32.9 g), Protein 0.1 g

SPIRULINA

SUPER CITRUS

MANGO MOJO

BAR VARIATIONS

POMEGRANATE MARGARITA GELS
Prepare as directed using cranberry-pomegranate juice as the fruit juice and 1 tablespoon fresh lime juice in place of the lemon juice.

SPIRULINA GELS
Add 2 teaspoons spirulina powder along with the lemon juice.

SUPER CITRUS GELS
Prepare as directed using 1/2 cup pulp-free orange juice and 1/2 cup fresh lemon or lime juice.

MANGO MOJO GELS
Prepare as directed using mango nectar as the fruit juice and 2 teaspoons fresh lime juice in place of the lemon juice.

MOCHA-MOTION GELS
Prepare as directed using apple juice as the fruit juice and adding 1 1/2 tablespoons instant espresso powder and 1 tablespoon unsweetened, natural cocoa powder to the mixture before heating.

BOMBASTIC BERRY GELS
Prepare as directed using mixed berry juice as the fruit juice.

LUCY BARS

(COMPARE TO _LÄRABAR®_)

The first thing I do at the beginning of each week is make a batch (or two, or three) of these bars. They've become a staple in my family's diet and have sustained us on countless trips, fitness treks, and busy days. I predict they will become a standard in your diet, too. After all, who doesn't love a delicious recipe that (a) has a minimal ingredient list; (b) requires no cooking; and (c) can be squished into lunchboxes, pockets, fanny packs, and backpacks for hours (umm, even days) on end? With all of the great options for dried fruits, nuts, and seeds, the possibilities for variation are boundless, and if you buy your ingredients in bulk (please do! The savings are substantial), the cost per bar is minimal, too. This starter template is for cherry pie bars (my all-time favorite); you can start with any variation from the list or from your own imagination. **MAKES 6 BARS**

DARK CHOCOLATE BROWNIE

CARROT CAKE

BLUEBERRY COBBLER

CHERRY PIE

1 cup packed dried cherries

1/4 cup packed pitted, soft dates

1 cup warm water

1 cup raw almonds

1/4 teaspoon ground cinnamon

1/8 teaspoon fine sea salt (optional)

1. Line a 9 by 5-inch loaf pan with plastic wrap and spray with nonstick cooking spray.

2. Combine the cherries, dates, and warm water in a small bowl. Let stand for 5 to 10 minutes until the fruit is soft (time will vary according to the dryness of the fruit). Drain and pat dry with paper towels.

3. Meanwhile, place the almonds in a food processor and process until finely chopped (but not a paste). Add the drained fruit, cinnamon, and salt (if using). Process, using on/off pulses, until the fruit is finely chopped and blended and the mixture begins to stick together and clump on the sides of the bowl.

4. Transfer the mixture to the prepared pan. Place a large piece of parchment paper, wax paper, or plastic wrap (coated with nonstick cooking spray) atop the bar mixture and use it to spread and flatten the mixture evenly in the pan; leave the paper or plastic wrap to cover. Refrigerate for 30 minutes.

5. Using the liner, lift the mixture from the pan and transfer to a cutting board. Uncover and cut into 6 bars.

BAR TIPS

—If the dried fruit you are using is already super-soft and moist, you can skip the soaking step.

—Whole dates are best for this recipe, but if pre-chopped is what you have (or all that you can find), you can still use them. One caveat: chopped dates are typically coated with oat flour and/or sugar. The coating can be removed with the soaking, but soak them separately from any other dried fruit you choose to use; because they are pre-chopped, they will only need 2 to 3 minutes of soaking. If they are left to soak for too long, they will begin to disintegrate.

—Form the mixture into any size or shape you like, such as balls or mini bars.

BAR KEEPING

Tightly wrap the bars individually in plastic wrap.

ROOM TEMP: 3 days
REFRIGERATOR: 3 weeks
FREEZER: 3 months in airtight container; thaw 1 hour

APRICOT AMBROSIA

CHERRY PIE

ORIGINAL RECIPE

1 cup packed dried cherries

1/4 cup packed pitted, soft dates

1 cup warm water

1 cup raw almonds

1/4 teaspoon ground cinnamon

1/8 teaspoon fine sea salt (optional)

BAR VARIATIONS

APPLE PIE BARS

Replace the cherries with an equal amount of dried apples and the almonds with an equal amount of raw pecans or walnuts. Increase the cinnamon to 1 1/2 teaspoons.

KEY LIME PIE BARS

Omit the cherries and increase the dates to 1 cup. Replace the almonds with an equal amount of raw cashews and omit the cinnamon. Add 1/3 cup unsweetened flake or shredded coconut, 2 tablespoons fresh lime juice, and 2 teaspoons finely grated lime zest to the processor along with the nuts.

LEMON PIE BARS

Omit the cherries and increase the dates to 1 1/4 cups. Replace half of the almonds with 1/2 cup of raw cashews and omit the cinnamon. Add 2 tablespoons fresh lemon juice and 2 teaspoons finely grated lemon zest to the processor along with the nuts.

COCONUT CREAM PIE BARS

Omit the cherries and increase the dates to 1 cup. Replace the almonds with an equal amount of raw cashews and omit the cinnamon. Add 1/2 cup unsweetened flake or shredded coconut to the processor along with the nuts.

CASHEW OR PEANUT COOKIE DOUGH BARS

Omit the cherries and increase the dates to 1 1/4 cups. Replace the almonds with an equal amount of raw cashews or raw peanuts and omit the cinnamon. If desired, add 3 tablespoons bittersweet or semisweet chocolate chips to the processor along with the nuts.

PECAN PIE BARS

Omit the cherries and increase the dates to 1 1/4 cups. Reduce the total amount of almonds to 1/4 cup, add 3/4 cup pecans, and omit the cinnamon.

GINGERBREAD BARS

Omit the cherries and increase the dates to 1 1/4 cups and replace half of the almonds with 1/2 cup of pecans. Increase the total amount of cinnamon to 1/2 teaspoon and add 3/4 teaspoon ground ginger and 1/8 teaspoon ground cloves to the processor along with the nuts.

PB & J BARS

Decrease the total amount of cherries to 1/2 cup and increase the dates to 3/4 cup. Replace the almonds with an equal amount of peanuts (raw or roasted) and omit the cinnamon.

CAPPUCCINO BARS

Omit the cherries and increase the dates to 1 1/4 cups. Reduce the almonds to 1/2 cup and add 1/2 cup raw cashews. Add 1 tablespoon roasted coffee beans and 1/2 teaspoon vanilla extract along with the nuts.

Nutrients per bar: Calories 183, Fat 8 g, (Saturated 0.6 g), Cholesterol 0 mg, Sodium 3 mg, Carbs 27.8 g (Fiber 3.4 g, Sugars 19.4 g), Protein 4.3 g

TROPICAL ESCAPE BARS

Replace the cherries with an equal amount of dried, unsweetened pineapple and the almonds with an equal amount of raw cashews. Omit the dates and cinnamon. Add 1/4 cup dried, unsweetened flake or shredded coconut and 1 tablespoon finely grated tangerine or orange zest along with the cashews.

OATMEAL RAISIN COOKIE BARS

Replace the cherries with an equal amount of raisins and omit the dates. Replace the almonds with 3/4 cup old-fashioned or quick-cooking rolled oats and 3/4 cup raw cashews. Increase the cinnamon to 1/2 teaspoon.

BLUEBERRY COBBLER BARS

Replace the cherries with an equal amount of dried blueberries. Replace the almonds with 3/4 cup walnuts or pecans and 1/2 cup old-fashioned rolled oats. Add 1/2 teaspoon finely grated lemon zest.

DARK CHOCOLATE BROWNIE BARS

Omit the cherries and increase the dates to 1 cup. Reduce the almonds to 1/2 cup and add 1/2 cup walnuts. Add 3 tablespoons bittersweet or semisweet chocolate chips and 2 tablespoons unsweetened cocoa powder along with the almonds. Omit the cinnamon.

CARROT CAKE BARS

Replace the dates and cherries with a combination of 1/2 cup dates, 1/4 cup raisins, and 1/4 cup dried, unsweetened pineapple. Replace the almonds with an equal amount of walnuts. Add 1/4 cup peeled, shredded carrots, 1/4 cup unsweetened flake or shredded coconut, and 2 teaspoons coconut oil.

APRICOT AMBROSIA BARS

Replace the dates and cherries with 1 1/4 cups dried apricots. Reduce the almonds to 2/3 cup and add 1/2 cup unsweetened flake or shredded coconut to the process along with the nuts.

MOONBEAM BARS

(COMPARE TO *LUNA*® BARS)

2 1/3 cups crisp brown rice cereal

1/2 cup quick-cooking rolled oats

1/4 cup finely chopped dried
cranberries or cherries

1/3 cup natural, unsweetened nut or
seed butter (e.g., almond, cashew,
or sunflower)

1/3 cup DIY Glucose Syrup (see page
30), organic light corn syrup, or
brown rice syrup

1/4 cup lightly packed all-natural,
sweetened vanilla vegan or whey
protein powder

2 teaspoons finely grated orange zest

1/8 teaspoon fine sea salt

White Chocolate Bar Coating (see
page 31)

If nutty, crunchy, crispiness is your idea of the perfect pick-me-up, I've got just what the doctor ordered. That's right, the doctor ordered power bars. The brown crisp rice base renders the bars light and crisp, while the additions of oats and protein power lend enough substance to stave off hunger for hours. Nut (or seed) butter adds depth and subtle natural sweetness, and of course a thin schmear of white chocolate, dark chocolate, or Greek yogurt coating tops things off in the most delicious way (you could leave it off...but why?). **MAKES 10 BARS**

1. Line an 8-inch square baking pan with foil or parchment paper and spray with nonstick cooking spray.

2. Stir together the cereal, oats, and cranberries in a large bowl.

3. In a small saucepan, combine the nut or seed butter and syrup. Heat over medium-low, stirring, for 2 to 4 minutes until mixture is melted and bubbly. Remove from heat and slowly whisk in the protein powder, orange zest, and salt until blended.

4. Immediately pour the nut or seed butter mixture over the cereal mixture, mixing with a spatula until coated.

5. Transfer the mixture to the prepared pan. Place a large piece of parchment paper, wax paper, or plastic wrap (coated with nonstick cooking spray) atop the bar mixture and use it to spread, flatten, and very firmly compact the mixture evenly in the pan. Cool at least 1 hour until firmly set.

6. Spread or drizzle the bar coating over the cooled mixture. Refrigerate for at least 30 minutes until the chocolate is set.

7. Using the liner, lift the mixture from the pan and transfer to a cutting board. Uncover and cut into 10 bars.

BAR TIPS

—I mean it when I say firmly compact the bars. Press, press, press, and then press again! Thirty seconds of effort will pay off with bars that hold together every time.

—If you don't want to use protein powder, you don't have to; simply increase the total amount of oats by 2 tablespoons. Alternatively, you can add 2 tablespoons of flaxseed meal or 3 tablespoons of nonfat instant milk powder.

BAR KEEPING

Tightly wrap the bars individually in plastic wrap.

ROOM TEMP: 2 days
REFRIGERATOR: 2 weeks
FREEZER: 3 months in airtight container; thaw 1/2 hour

Nutrients per bar: Calories 177, Fat 6.1 g, (Saturated 1.8 g), Cholesterol 6 mg, Sodium 91 mg, Carbs 26.2 g (Fiber 1.1 g, Sugars 15.5 g), Protein 6.3 g

BAR VARIATIONS

ZESTY LEMON OR LIME BARS

Prepare as directed but omit the cranberries; use any flavor nut or seed butter except peanut. Use 2 teaspoons finely grated lemon or lime zest in place of the orange zest. Add 1 tablespoon fresh lemon or lime juice along with the salt. Use the White Chocolate Bar Coating (see page 31).

JOY OF ALMOND BARS

Use almond butter for the nut butter and omit the cranberries and orange zest. Reduce the total amount of crisp rice cereal to 2 cups and to it add 1/2 cup unsweetened flake or shredded coconut, chopped. Add 3/4 teaspoon almond extract along with the salt. Use the Chocolate Bar Coating (see page 31).

CHOCOLATE-COVERED CANDY CANE BARS

Use any flavor nut or seed butter except peanut. Omit the cranberries and orange zest and add 1 teaspoon pure peppermint extract along with the salt. Use either the Chocolate Bar Coating or White Chocolate Bar Coating (see page 31).

WHITE CHOCOLATE MACADAMIA BARS

Use any flavor nut or seed butter except peanut and omit the cranberries and orange zest. Reduce the total amount of crisp rice cereal to 2 cups and to it add 1/4 cup roasted macadamia nuts, chopped. Add 1 teaspoon pure maple extract along with the salt. Use the White Chocolate Bar Coating (see page 31).

DOUBLE CHOCOLATE BARS

Prepare as directed, but omit the cranberries and orange zest. Use an equal amount of lightly packed all-natural, sweetened chocolate protein powder in place of vanilla. Add 1 tablespoon natural, unsweetened cocoa powder along with the salt. Use the Chocolate or White Chocolate Bar Coating (see page 31).

ACTIVITY
BARS

Complex carbohydrates never tasted more delicious than in these activity bars. Think of them as a terrific choice whenever you need a healthy power boost: simply pack in your purse, briefcase, lunchbox, or gym bag for some perfectly-portioned power on the go. These bars are great before, during, or after physical activities, and they also make great between-meal snacks because they can help your blood sugar levels (and therefore your energy levels) remain stable throughout the day. In other words, say goodbye to mid-day crashes as well as junk food cravings. Additionally, you may actually reduce your overall caloric intake by curbing overeating at your next meal.

BREWED AWAKENING CAPPUCCINO BARS

2 cups quick-cooking rolled oats

3/4 cup walnut halves, chopped

3/4 cup whole almonds, chopped

3/4 cup unsweetened flake or shredded coconut

1 1/4 cups crisp brown rice cereal

3/4 cup DIY Glucose Syrup (see page 30), organic light corn syrup, or brown rice syrup

1/2 cup natural cane sugar or packed organic light brown sugar

2 tablespoons water

1 tablespoon instant espresso powder

1/2 teaspoon fine sea salt

1/2 teaspoon ground cinnamon

1 teaspoon vanilla extract

Coffee and breakfast all in one handy bar? Yes, ma'am! That's not to say you can't enjoy your favorite brew in tandem with your bar because you most certainly can. As an avowed coffee lover, I might go so far as to say that you should. These bars solve a conundrum: how does one make the morning coffee whilst too sleepy to make said morning coffee (or walk to the nearest café)? Answer: nibble one of these bars (half-opened eyes will suffice) as you measure, pour, and press the "on" button. You're welcome. **MAKES 16 BARS**

1. Line an 8-inch square baking pan with foil or parchment paper and spray with nonstick cooking spray.

2. Preheat oven to 350°F.

3. Spread the oats, walnuts, almonds, and coconut on a large rimmed baking sheet. Bake in the preheated oven for 6 to 8 minutes, shaking halfway through, until golden and fragrant. Transfer to a large bowl; stir in the cereal.

4. Meanwhile, combine the syrup, sugar, water, espresso powder, and salt in a small saucepan. Heat over medium-low, stirring, for 5 to 6 minutes until the sugar is dissolved and the mixture is bubbly. Remove from heat and stir in the cinnamon and vanilla.

5. Immediately pour syrup mixture over the nut mixture, mixing with a spatula until coated.

6. Transfer the mixture to the prepared pan. Place a large piece of parchment paper, wax paper, or plastic wrap (coated with nonstick cooking spray) atop the bar mixture and use it to spread, flatten, and very firmly compact the mixture evenly in the pan. Cool at least 1 hour until firmly set.

7. Using the liner, lift the mixture from the pan and transfer to a cutting board. Cut into 16 bars.

Nutrients per bar: Calories 220, Fat 9.7 g, (Saturated 2.2 g), Cholesterol 0 mg, Sodium 98 mg, Carbs 31.3 g (Fiber 2.1 g, Sugars 20.1 g), Protein 5 g

BAR TIPS

—Other grain flakes work beautifully in these bars. Bump up the protein with an equal amount of quinoa flakes in place of the oats, or use an equal amount of spelt, rye, rice, or kamut flakes.

—*Don't be tempted to cut back on or play around with the sweeteners; you can do that with many bars, but not this one.* In the absence of other binding ingredients like coconut oil or nut butter, the sweeteners here are working solo to hold these bars together. It may seem like a generous amount of sweetener at first glance, but these are dense bars that get cut into sixteen pieces, which literally equals a tablespoon of sweetener per bar. And yes, the combination of dry and liquid sweeteners is essential; tinker around and you'll end up with cappuccino crumble instead of bars.

—1 1/2 tablespoons instant coffee powder (regular or decaffeinated) may be used in place of the espresso powder.

BAR KEEPING

Tightly wrap the bars individually in plastic wrap.

ROOM TEMP: 3 days
REFRIGERATOR: 2 weeks
FREEZER: 3 months in airtight container; thaw 1 hour

BAR VARIATIONS

CAPPUCCINO CHIP BARS
Add 1/3 cup miniature semisweet or bittersweet chocolate chips to the mixture before transferring to the pan.

ALMOND TOFFEE BARS
Omit the walnuts and increase the total amount of almonds to 2 cups. Omit the espresso powder and cinnamon and use an equal amount of packed organic dark brown sugar in place of the cane sugar.

PROTEIN JAVA JOLT BARS
Prepare as directed but omit the coconut and add 1/2 cup all-natural, sweetened vanilla or chocolate vegan or whey protein powder.

TURKISH COFFEE BARS
Prepare as directed, but replace the cinnamon with 3/4 teaspoon ground cardamom.

COCONUT PECAN PIE BARS
Use 2 cups pecan halves in place of the walnut and almonds. Omit the espresso powder and cinnamon and use an equal amount of packed organic dark brown sugar in place of the cane sugar.

CRISPY KALE BARS

CRISPY KALE LEAVES

1 large bunch kale, tough stems and center ribs removed, torn into bite-sized pieces

1 tablespoon vegetable oil

BARS

1 cup quick-cooking rolled oats

1/3 cup pepitas (green pumpkin seeds) or sunflower seeds

3 tablespoons sesame seeds

1 cup unsweetened whole-grain puffed cereal (e.g., puffed wheat, quinoa, or rice)

1/3 cup goji berries, dried cherries, or dried cranberries, coarsely chopped

1/3 cup natural, unsweetened nut or seed butter (e.g., almond, cashew, or sunflower)

1/4 cup natural cane sugar or packed organic light brown sugar

1/4 cup DIY Glucose Syrup (see page 30), organic light corn syrup, or brown rice syrup

1/4 teaspoon fine sea salt

1/4 teaspoon almond extract

Copious amounts of kale were sacrificed in my pursuit of a kale energy bar. On my umpteenth attempt at puréeing the leaves into gooey-green glue, inspiration struck: why not incorporate the kale in crispy kale-chip form? It only took one batch to know I had a winner. The trick to getting great bars is to make sure that the kale is super-crisp, which is a cinch so long as you dry the leaves thoroughly—I'm talking layers of clean dish towels or many turns in the salad spinner, a mere minute or two of effort, before baking. If water remains on the leaves, the kale will steam, not crisp. I don't know about you, but the prospect of steamed kale bars doesn't do it for me. But crispy, toasted seed-enhanced bars? Yes and yes!

MAKES 10 BARS

1. Line an 8-inch square baking pan with foil or parchment paper and spray with nonstick cooking spray.

2. Preheat oven to 350°F.

3. To prepare the kale: Thoroughly wash the kale under cold water and then remove all of the excess moisture by blotting the leaves between several layers of paper towels or spinning multiple times in a salad spinner. Transfer the kale to a parchment-lined baking sheet. Drizzle the leaves with the oil, tossing to coat the leaves.

4. Bake the kale in the preheated oven for 12-17 minutes until the leaves appear paper-thin and crisp, but not browned (watch closely). Using the parchment liner, transfer the kale to a rack and cool completely, about 10 minutes.

5. Meanwhile, spread the oats, pepitas, and sesame seeds on a large rimmed baking sheet. Bake in the preheated oven for 5 to 8 minutes, shaking halfway through, until golden and fragrant. Transfer to a large bowl; stir in cereal and berries. Crumble the cooled kale leaves into the bowl; gently stir to combine.

6. Combine the nut or seed butter, sugar, syrup, and salt in a small saucepan. Heat over medium-low, stirring, for 4 to 5 minutes until the sugar is dissolved and the mixture is bubbly. Remove from heat and stir in the almond extract.

7. Immediately pour the syrup mixture over the oats mixture, mixing with a spatula until coated.

Nutrients per bar: Calories 205, Fat 8.5 g, (Saturated 1.4 g), Cholesterol 0 mg, Sodium 102 mg, Carbs 29.3 g (Fiber 2.5 g, Sugars 15.8 g), Protein 5.8 g

8. Transfer the mixture to the prepared pan. Place a large piece of parchment paper, wax paper, or plastic wrap (coated with nonstick cooking spray) atop the bar mixture and use it to spread, flatten, and very firmly compact the mixture evenly in the pan. Refrigerate at least 1 hour until firmly set.

9. Using the liner, lift the mixture from the pan and transfer to a cutting board. Cut into 10 bars.

BAR TIPS

—For best results, do not use peanut butter; it will overwhelm the other flavors in the bars.

—The ratio of dry and liquid sweeteners here is essential for binding the bars— experiment at your own risk!

—The crispy kale leaves can be prepared up to 1 day ahead. Cool completely and store in an airtight container until ready to use.

BAR KEEPING

Tightly wrap the bars individually in plastic wrap.

ROOM TEMP: 2 days
REFRIGERATOR: 1 week
FREEZER: 3 months in airtight container; thaw 1/2 hour

BAR VARIATION

CRISPY SPINACH & APRICOT BARS
Prepare as directed, but use 6 cups of packed baby spinach leaves in place of the kale and an equal amount of chopped dried apricots in place of the dried berries. Omit the almond extract and add 1 1/2 teaspoons finely grated orange zest instead.

CARROT CAKE ACTION BARS

2 1/4 cups old-fashioned or quick-cooking rolled oats

1/3 cup natural cane sugar or packed organic light brown sugar

2 teaspoons pumpkin pie spice

1/2 teaspoon baking soda

1/4 teaspoon fine sea salt

2 large eggs

1/4 cup pure maple syrup, agave nectar, or honey

1/4 cup virgin coconut oil, warmed until melted, or vegetable oil

1 teaspoon vanilla extract

1 cup peeled, finely shredded carrots

1/2 cup unsweetened flake or shredded coconut

1/2 cup raisins, dried currants, or dried cranberries

1/2 cup chopped, toasted walnuts or pecans

Greek Yogurt Bar Coating or White Chocolate Bar Coating (optional; see page 31)

When you want carrot cake but (a) you're about to go for a 10-mile run; (b) you just got back from a 10-mile run; or (c) you're still in bed because you decided it was too cold to go for a 10-mile run, then...(action music)...it's Carrot Cake Action Bars to the rescue! Subtly spiced with cozy nuances of maple and coconut, nutty bits of toasted walnuts, and sweet raisins—they will easily satisfy your carrot-y cravings. Carrots may not get much superfood buzz, but they should, because they are crazy good for you: colossal levels of vitamin A (beta-carotene is named after carrots) as well as high levels of fiber, vitamin C, vitamin K, and multiple minerals. MAKES 12 BARS

1. Line a 9-inch square baking pan with foil or parchment paper and spray with nonstick cooking spray.

2. Preheat oven to 350°F.

3. Mix together the oats, sugar, pumpkin pie spice, baking soda, and salt in a large bowl.

4. Mix the eggs, maple syrup, oil, and vanilla in a small bowl until blended.

5. Add the egg mixture to the oats mixture and stir until just blended. Mix in the carrots, coconut, raisins, and walnuts.

6. Spread the batter evenly in the prepared pan.

7. Bake in the preheated oven for 35 to 40 minutes or until top is golden brown and a toothpick inserted in the center comes out clean. Transfer to a wire rack and cool completely.

8. Using the liner, lift the mixture from the pan and transfer to a cutting board. Cut into 12 bars. If desired, drizzle or spread with bar coating. Store in the refrigerator or freezer.

Nutrients per bar: Calories 228, Fat 11.4 g, (Saturated 3.2 g), Cholesterol 31 mg, Sodium 73 mg, Carbs 29.1 g (Fiber 2.4 g, Sugars 16.1 g), Protein 4.8 g

BAR TIP

—No pumpkin pie spice? No problem. You can make your own by combining 1 teaspoon ground cinnamon, 1/2 teaspoon ground ginger, 1/4 teaspoon ground nutmeg, and 1/4 teaspoon ground cloves to replace the 2 teaspoons of pumpkin pie spice.

BAR KEEPING

Tightly wrap the bars individually in plastic wrap.

REFRIGERATOR: 1 week
FREEZER: 3 months in airtight container; thaw 1 hour

BAR VARIATIONS

VEGAN CARROT CAKE BARS
Use agave nectar or maple syrup for the sweetener and replace the egg with 2 tablespoons flaxseed meal mixed with 1/4 cup warm water. Let the flaxseed mixture stand for 5 minutes before using.

FRESH APPLE ACTION BARS
Replace the carrots with an equal amount of peeled, shredded tart apples (e.g., Granny Smith; about 2 large).

INDIAN SPICE CARROT BARS
Replace the pumpkin pie spice with 1 teaspoon ground cardamom and use honey for the sweetener. Use golden raisins in place of the dark raisins and use an equal amount of chopped, roasted pistachios in place of the walnuts.

PUMPED UP CARROT BARS
Prepare as directed but reduce the total amout of oats to 1 3/4 cups and add 1/2 cup all-natural, sweetened vanilla vegan or whey protein powder.

CITRUS-SEED-FRUIT BARS

3/4 cup pepitas (green pumpkin seeds)

1/4 cup sunflower seeds

1/4 cup sesame seeds

2 teaspoons finely grated orange zest

1 teaspoon finely grated lemon zest

3 tablespoons orange juice

2 tablespoons fresh lemon juice

1/4 cup chia seeds

3/4 cup dried apricots

3/4 cup chopped soft dried figs or dates

1/4 teaspoon fine sea salt

Like a perfectly balanced day, workout, or backpack (yes, backpack; if you've ever schlepped a cattywampus one for hours on end, you can understand the happiness that a symmetrical backpack brings), these bars have elements of harmony and contrast that come together beautifully. Think crunchy seeds and moist golden dried fruits, plus flavors that range from sweet to savory to sour to earthy. These make a fabulous option when you feel you've had one chocolate nut butter bar too many. **MAKES 10 BARS**

1. Line an 8-inch square baking pan with foil or parchment paper and spray with nonstick cooking spray.

2. Preheat oven to 300°F.

3. Spread the pepitas, sunflower seeds, and sesame seeds on a large rimmed baking sheet. Bake in the preheated oven for 8 to 11 minutes, shaking halfway through, until golden and fragrant. Transfer to the bowl of a food processor and cool completely.

4. Meanwhile, combine the orange zest, lemon zest, orange juice, lemon juice, and chia seeds in a small bowl. Let stand for 5 to 6 minutes until the mixture begins to gel.

5. Add the apricots and figs to the seeds in the food processor; pulse a few times until coarsely chopped. Add the chia mixture and salt; process, using on/off pulses, until the mixture begins to stick together, but is not a paste.

6. Transfer the mixture to the prepared pan. Place a large piece of parchment paper, wax paper, or plastic wrap (coated with nonstick cooking spray) atop the bar mixture and use it to spread, flatten, and compact the mixture evenly in the pan. Discard the paper or plastic.

7. Bake in the preheated oven for 14 to 17 minutes or until the top of the mixture appears somewhat dry. Transfer to a wire rack and cool completely.

8. Using the liner, lift the mixture from the pan and transfer to a cutting board. Refrigerate the mixture for 30 minutes or until completely chilled. Cut into 10 bars. Store in the refrigerator or freezer.

Nutrients per bar: Calories 105, Fat 3.3 g, (Saturated 0 g), Cholesterol 0 mg, Sodium 61 mg, Carbs 19.1 g (Fiber 1.6 g, Sugars 13.4 g), Protein 2 g

BAR TIPS

—An equal amount of flaxseed meal may be used in place of the chia seeds, or simply up the total amount of sesame seeds or sunflower seeds by another 1/4 cup.

—The bars may look as if they will not hold together when you first take them out of the oven. If you make sure they are completely chilled before you try to cut them, they hold together perfectly.

BAR KEEPING

Tightly wrap the bars individually in plastic wrap.

REFRIGERATOR: 1 week
FREEZER: 3 months in airtight container; thaw 1 hour

BAR VARIATIONS

CARDAMOM FIG BARS
Replace the pepitas, sunflower seeds, and sesame seeds with 1 1/2 cups walnuts. Omit the apricots and instead, use a total 1 1/2 cups chopped soft dried figs. Add 3/4 teaspoon ground cardamom along with the salt.

MOROCCAN FRUIT AND SPICE BARS
Replace the pepitas and sunflower seeds with 1 cup whole almonds. Replace the figs with 3/4 cup chopped soft prunes. Add 1 teaspoon ground cinnamon along with the salt.

CARROT CAKE
ACTION BARS

RECIPE
PAGE
60

CITRUS-SEED-
FRUIT BARS

RECIPE
PAGE
62

GREEN TEA & GINGER BARS

RECIPE
PAGE
66

GREEN TEA & GINGER BARS

1 1/3 cups roasted, lightly salted pistachios or cashews, coarsely chopped

1/2 cup quick-cooking rolled oats

1/2 cup crisp brown rice cereal

2/3 cup packed golden raisins or chopped dried apricots

1/3 cup DIY Glucose Syrup (see page 30), organic light corn syrup, or brown rice syrup

1 1/2 tablespoons green tea powder (matcha)

1 teaspoon finely grated lime zest

2 teaspoons fresh lime juice

1 teaspoon ground ginger

"Let's have tea!" is my family's code for "let's eat cookies!" We love a good cuppa, including green teas, and a gingery tea cookie in accompaniment is hard to beat. I think you know where this is going. Since we're also a family that loves to eat well and stay fit, it was only a matter of time before I began experimenting with tea in my power bars. These green beauties are first in show from my trials. Matcha—finely milled Japanese green tea powder—is the unrivaled bar star here. Unlike regular black tea or green tea, matcha isn't fermented (oxidized) at all, but rather steamed immediately and ground into a powder. The result is a brilliant emerald powder with stellar levels of antioxidants, chlorophyll, and other nutrients. Let's have tea, indeed. **MAKES 12 BARS**

1. Line an 8-inch square baking pan with foil or parchment paper and spray with nonstick cooking spray.

2. Preheat oven to 325°F.

3. Stir together the pistachios, oats, cereal, and raisins in a large bowl.

4. Combine the syrup, matcha, lime zest, lime juice, and ginger in a small bowl until blended.

5. Pour the syrup mixture over the pistachio mixture, mixing with a spatula until coated.

6. Transfer the mixture to the prepared pan. Place a large piece of parchment paper, wax paper, or plastic wrap (coated with nonstick cooking spray) atop the bar mixture and use it to spread, flatten, and very firmly compact the mixture evenly in the pan. Discard the paper or plastic.

7. Bake in the preheated oven for 20 to 24 minutes or until golden at the edges. Immediately press down the mixture with the back of a spatula to further compact the bars. Let cool 10 minutes in the pan on a wire rack.

8. Using the liner, lift the mixture from the pan and transfer to a cutting board. Cut into 12 bars and cool completely before peeling off liner.

Nutrients per bar: Calories 157, Fat 7.3 g, (Saturated 1.4 g), Cholesterol 0 mg, Sodium 16 mg, Carbs 22.5 g (Fiber 1.1 g, Sugars 13.4 g), Protein 3.1 g

BAR TIPS

—If matcha is unavailable, use 1 1/2 tablespoons of loose-leaf green tea leaves, finely crumbled, in its place. The bars will not have the bright green color that the matcha delivers, but they will still have a delicious and healthy dose of green tea goodness.

—Equal amounts of lemon zest and lemon juice can be used in place of the lime zest and juice.

BAR KEEPING

Tightly wrap the bars individually in plastic wrap.

ROOM TEMP: 3 days
REFRIGERATOR: 2 weeks
FREEZER: 3 months in airtight container; thaw 1 hour

BAR VARIATIONS

ENGLISH BREAKFAST BARS
Use 1 1/2 tablespoons of black tea leaves, finely crumbled, in place of the matcha. Use an equal amount of roasted, lightly salted almonds, chopped, in place of the pistachios and an equal amount of dried currants or dark raisins in place of the golden raisins. Replace the lime zest and juice with lemon zest and juice. Replace the ginger with an equal amount of pumpkin pie spice.

CHAI BREAKFAST BARS
Use 1 1/2 tablespoons of black tea leaves, finely crumbled, in place of the matcha. Use an equal amount of toasted pecans in place of the pistachios and an equal amount of chopped dates or raisins in places of the golden raisins. Use 1 teaspoon vanilla extract in place of the lime zest and juice and add 1 teaspoon pumpkin pie spice along with the ginger.

MORNING MAPLE BARS

2 cups old-fashioned or quick-
  cooking rolled oats

1/2 cup pecans, chopped

1 cup dried fruit (e.g., blueberries,
  cherries, raisins)

1/2 cup low-fat milk or plain nondairy
  milk

1/2 cup multigrain hot cereal

1 cup natural, unsweetened nut or
  seed butter (e.g., almond, cashew,
  or sunflower)

1/2 cup pure maple syrup

1/4 teaspoon fine sea salt

1 teaspoon pure maple extract
  (optional)

Crisp-chewy, scented with maple, and stuffed with dried fruit and grains, there is so much to love about these bars. Dried fruit is a great source of concentrated energy, and, along with the oats and multigrain cereal, is an excellent source of fiber. The protein from the oats, milk, nuts, and nut butter is not too shabby, either. Heed my advice and declare any time of the day morning-time. **MAKES 16 BARS**

1. Line an 8-inch square baking pan with foil or parchment paper and spray with nonstick cooking spray.

2. Preheat oven to 350°F.

3. Spread the oats and pecans on a large rimmed baking sheet. Bake in the preheated oven for 6 to 8 minutes, shaking halfway through, until golden and fragrant. Transfer to a large bowl.

4. Place the dried fruit in a food processor and process until finely chopped (but not a paste). Transfer to the bowl with the oats mixture.

5. Bring the milk to a boil in a small saucepan set over medium heat. Stir in the cereal and remove from the heat; let stand for 2 minutes. Add the nut or seed butter, maple syrup, and salt. Cook and stir the mixture over low heat for 7 minutes; remove from the heat and stir in maple extract, if using.

6. Immediately add the cereal mixture to the oats mixture, mixing with a spatula until coated.

7. Transfer the mixture to the prepared pan. Place a large piece of parchment paper, wax paper, or plastic wrap (coated with nonstick cooking spray) atop the bar mixture and use it to spread, flatten, and very firmly compact the mixture evenly in the pan. Cool completely and let stand at least 2 hours until firm.

8. Using the liner, lift the mixture from the pan and transfer to a cutting board. Cut into 16 bars.

Nutrients per bar: Calories 240, Fat 13 g, (Saturated 3.4 g), Cholesterol 0 mg, Sodium 42 mg, Carbs 26.4 g (Fiber 3.2 g, Sugars 12.7 g), Protein 7.4 g

BAR TIPS

—Although peanut butter works perfectly well in this recipe, it can overwhelm the flavor of the maple syrup. For a more pronounced maple flavor, opt for a milder-flavored nut or seed butter such as almond, sunflower seed, or cashew.

—Toasting the oats and pecans adds tremendous flavor, but if you are in a hurry, you can skip this step.

BAR KEEPING

Tightly wrap the bars individually in plastic wrap.

ROOM TEMP: 3 days
REFRIGERATOR: 1 week
FREEZER: 3 months in airtight container; thaw 1 hour

BAR VARIATION

HONEY, GET GOING! APRICOT BARS
Use an equal amount of honey in place of the maple syrup, an equal amount of whole almonds, chopped, in place of the pecans, and an equal amount of vanilla extract in place of the maple extract. Use chopped dried apricots for the dried fruit.

CRISPY-CHEWY CHERRY-FLAX PUCKS

2/3 cup ground flaxseed meal

1/2 cup natural, unsweetened almond butter

1/3 cup pure maple syrup, honey, or agave nectar

1/3 cup plain almond milk

1/2 teaspoon almond extract

2/3 cup dried cherries

Almond butter not only makes these pucks delicious, but also delivers a significant nutritional boost: it's high in protein and rich in vitamin E, a powerful antioxidant that helps protect cells from oxidative stress, which has been linked to heart disease and Alzheimer's. **MAKES 12 PUCKS**

1. Lightly spray a 12-cup muffin pan with nonstick cooking spray.

2. Preheat oven to 325°F.

3. In a large bowl, whisk together the flaxseed meal, almond butter, maple syrup, milk, and almond extract until well combined. Stir in cherries until just combined.

4. Evenly divide the batter into the prepared muffin cups.

5. Bake in preheated oven for 25 to 30 minutes or until edges are golden brown and tops appear somewhat dry. Let cool in the pan on a wire rack for 5 minutes, then transfer the pucks directly to the rack to cool completely.

BAR TIPS

—These pucks can be varied multiple ways. For example, use any variety of unsweetened, natural nut or seed butter, any variety of plain dairy or nondairy milk, or any variety of dried fruit in place of the cherries. Additionally, you can add up to 1/4 teaspoon of your favorite spice (e.g., ground cinnamon, cardamom, ginger, or allspice) or use vanilla extract in place of the almond extract.

BAR KEEPING

Tightly wrap the pucks individually in plastic wrap.

ROOM TEMP: 3 days
REFRIGERATOR: 1 week
FREEZER: 3 months in airtight container; thaw 1 hour

Nutrients per puck: Calories 161, Fat 8.1 g, (Saturated 1.3 g), Cholesterol 0 mg, Sodium 11 mg, Carbs 16.2 g (Fiber 4.3 g, Sugars 13.2 g), Protein 6.1 g

BAR VARIATIONS

CHOCOLATE CHIP ORANGE PUCKS
Replace the cherries with 1/2 cup miniature semisweet chocolate chips and replace the almond extract with 1 1/2 teaspoons finely grated orange zest.

DOUBLE CHOCOLATE FLAX PUCKS
Reduce the flaxseed meal to 1/2 cup and increase the milk to 1/2 cup. Add 2 tablespoons unsweetened cocoa powder along with the flaxseed meal, replace the almond extract with an equal amount of vanilla extract, and replace the cherries with 1/2 cup miniature semisweet chocolate chips.

BLUEBERRY GINGERBREAD PUCKS
Replace the almond extract with an equal amount of vanilla extract and replace the cherries with an equal amount of dried blueberries. Add 3/4 teaspoon ground ginger, 1/2 teaspoon ground cinnamon, and 1/8 teaspoon ground nutmeg or cloves.

HIGH PROTEIN PUCKS
Reduce the flaxseed meal to 1/3 cup and the honey to 1/4 cup. Omit the almond extract and increase the milk to 1/2 cup total. Add 1/3 cup lightly packed all-natural, sweetened vanilla vegan or whey protein powder along with the flaxseed meal. Use the dried cherries or any variety of dried fruit.

RAISIN BRAN BOLT BARS

1 1/2 cups raisins

2 1/2 cups 100% bran cereal (pellet-shaped)

1 cup old-fashioned or quick-cooking rolled oats

1/2 cup walnuts or pecans, preferably toasted

1/2 cup nonfat dry milk powder

3/4 teaspoon ground cinnamon

1/4 cup honey or agave nectar

2 large eggs

2 tablespoons virgin coconut oil or vegetable oil

1 teaspoon vanilla extract

1/4 teaspoon fine sea salt

With antioxidants from raisins, high fiber from bran and oats, omega-3 fatty acids from walnuts and flaxseeds, and protein from milk powder and eggs, these are definitely not your grandmother's raisin bran—unless your grandmother runs 10 miles each morning, which is entirely possible. Whichever the case, these dense and delicious bars have multi-generational appeal and are sure to sustain you through the most rigorous mornings with nary a thought of lunch. **MAKES 12 BARS**

1. Line a 9-inch square baking pan with foil or parchment paper and spray with nonstick cooking spray.

2. Preheat oven to 350°F.

3. Place the raisins, cereal, oats, walnuts, dry milk powder, and cinnamon in a food processor. Process, using on/off pulses, until the mixture is coarsely chopped. Add the honey, eggs, oil, vanilla extract, and salt. Process, using on/off pulses, until just combined.

4. Transfer the mixture to the prepared pan. Place a large piece of parchment paper, wax paper, or plastic wrap (coated with nonstick cooking spray) atop the bar mixture and use it to spread and flatten the mixture evenly in the pan. Discard the paper or plastic.

5. Bake in the preheated oven for 18 to 22 minutes or until the top of the mixture appears dry.

6. Using the liner, lift the mixture from the pan and transfer to a wire rack to cool for 15 minutes. Transfer to a cutting board and cut into 12 bars. Cool the bars completely before peeling off liner.

Nutrients per bar: Calories 203, Fat 7 g, (Saturated 0.9 g), Cholesterol 31 mg, Sodium 95 mg, Carbs 35.4 g (Fiber 6.7 g, Sugars 18.1 g), Protein 6.2 g

BAR TIPS

—Make these bars gluten-free by substituting an equal amount of plain rice bran (not rice bran cereal) for the wheat bran.

—Use the kind of bran cereal that looks like tiny pellets. If flake is all that you can find, or all that you have, crush it fine before measuring the 1 cup needed in the recipe.

—I haven't seen apricot, cranberry, or date bran in the cereal aisle, but that doesn't mean you can't use dried fruits other than raisins in these bars. In fact, it's a brilliant idea.

—No dry milk powder? No problem— simply omit it.

BAR KEEPING

Tightly wrap the bars individually in plastic wrap.

ROOM TEMP: 2 days
REFRIGERATOR: 1 week
FREEZER: 3 months in airtight container; thaw 1 hour

BAR VARIATIONS

CRANBERRY SPICE BRAN BARS
Use an equal amount of dried cranberries in place of the raisins. Replace cinnamon with an equal amount of pumpkin pie spice.

POWERED-UP BRAN BARS
Omit the milk powder and reduce oats to 3/4 cup. Add 3/4 cup all-natural, sweetened vanilla vegan or whey protein powder along with the oats and cereal.

DOUBLE CHOCOLATE BRAN BARS
Use an equal amount of pitted, soft dates in place of the raisins and reduce oats to 3/4 cup. Add 1/3 cup of unsweetened, natural cocoa powder (not Dutch process). Omit the cinnamon. Sprinkle the bars with 1/2 cup miniature semisweet chocolate chips before baking.

HEALTHY HIPPY BARS

1 cup spelt flakes, quinoa flakes, or quick-cooking rolled oats

1 cup hemp hearts (shelled hemp seeds)

1/2 cup dried cherries

1/2 cup carob chips or semisweet chocolate chips

1/2 cup unsweetened flake or shredded coconut

2 tablespoons flaxseed meal

1/2 cup natural, unsweetened nut or seed butter (e.g., cashew, almond, or sunflower)

1/3 cup honey or agave nectar

1/4 teaspoon fine sea salt

I may appear straight-laced and sporty, but what lies beneath is a born-in-Berkeley, tie-dyed in the cotton hippy. It's most evident when it comes to my notions of comfort food: think whole grains, kale, nuts, seeds, organic fruit, granola, tofu, hummus, and lentils. Thank you, Mom and Dad. But, funny thing about these bars: despite my aim of creating an ode to hippy food in bar form—they comprise spelt, hemp, carob, and flaxseeds, for heaven's sake—everyone who tries them thinks they're eating an indulgent treat. I haven't the heart to tell them they're loading up on omega-3 fatty acids and whole grain fiber. Hippies are like that. **MAKES 12 BARS**

1. Line an 8-inch square baking pan with foil or parchment paper and spray with nonstick cooking spray.

2. Preheat oven to 325°F.

3. Place the spelt flakes, hemp hearts, cherries, carob chips, coconut, and flaxseed meal in a food processor. Process, using on/off pulses, until the mixture is finely chopped (but not a paste). Add the nut or seed butter, honey, and salt. Process, using on/off pulses, until just combined.

4. Transfer the mixture to the prepared pan. Place a large piece of parchment paper, wax paper, or plastic wrap (coated with nonstick cooking spray) atop the bar mixture and use it to spread and flatten the mixture evenly in the pan. Discard the paper or plastic.

5. Bake in the preheated oven for 20 to 24 minutes or until golden brown at the edges. Transfer to a wire rack and cool completely in the pan.

6. Using the liner, lift the mixture from the pan and transfer to a cutting board. Cut into 12 bars.

Nutrients per bar: Calories 189, Fat 10.4 g, (Saturated 3.3 g), Cholesterol 0 mg, Sodium 44 mg, Carbs 20.8 g (Fiber 2.4 g, Sugars 12.4 g), Protein 5.8 g

BAR TIPS

—If using spelt flakes, be sure to use flakes that resemble rolled oats, as opposed to ready-to-eat cereal that resembles corn flakes.

—Hemp hearts are softer than other seeds and have a flavor reminiscent of sunflower seeds, raw walnuts, or cashews; any of these makes a great substitute.

BAR KEEPING

Tightly wrap the bars individually in plastic wrap.

ROOM TEMP: 3 days
REFRIGERATOR: 2 weeks
FREEZER: 3 months in airtight container; thaw 1 hour

BAR VARIATION

FLOWER-POWER BARS
Omit the carob chips and use an equal amount of sunflower seeds (roasted or raw) in place of the hemp hearts. Use sunflower seed butter for the nut/seed butter and add 1 tablespoon finely grated lemon zest along with the salt.

BANANA SPLIT BARS

1/3 cup quinoa, rinsed

1/2 cup water

2 cups quick-cooking rolled oats

1 teaspoon ground cinnamon

1/2 teaspoon baking soda

1/2 teaspoon fine sea salt

1 1/2 cups mashed, very ripe bananas

1 large egg

1/4 cup honey, pure maple syrup, or agave nectar

1 tablespoon virgin coconut oil or vegetable oil

2 teaspoons vanilla extract

1/2 cup dried cherries, dried cranberries, or raisins

1/3 cup chopped toasted walnuts or pecans

1/4 cup miniature semisweet chocolate chips

I'm a no-frills banana bread kind of woman, but I simultaneously consider over-the-top banana splits a sign that God loves us. So although these heart-healthy bars are baked liked bread, the dried cherries, nuts, syrup, and chocolate chips allow me to ascribe them to the banana split camp. While they may taste indulgent, they are teeming with healthy goodness—fruits, nuts, whole grains, and antioxidants from the cinnamon and chocolate—to keep you going through your most active days. **MAKES 16 BARS**

1. Line a 9 by 13-inch baking pan with foil or parchment paper and spray with nonstick cooking spray.

2. Preheat oven to 325°F.

3. Combine the quinoa and water in a small saucepan. Bring to a boil over medium-high heat. Reduce heat to low, cover, and simmer for 9 to 13 minutes or until liquid is just barely absorbed. Remove from heat. Cover and let stand for 5 to 6 minutes. Remove the lid and fluff with a fork. Transfer to a medium bowl and cool completely.

4. Mix together the oats, cinnamon, baking soda, and salt in a large bowl.

5. Add the bananas, egg, honey, oil, and vanilla to the bowl of cooled quinoa, stirring until well blended.

6. Add the banana mixture to the oats mixture and stir until just blended. Mix in the cherries, walnuts, and chocolate chips.

7. Spread the batter evenly in the prepared pan.

8. Bake in the preheated oven for 25 to 30 minutes or until the top is golden brown and a toothpick inserted in the center comes out clean. Transfer to a wire rack and cool completely.

9. Using the liner, lift the mixture from the pan and transfer to a cutting board. Cut into 16 bars. Store in the refrigerator or freezer.

Nutrients per bar: Calories 143, Fat 4.4 g, (Saturated 1.1 g), Cholesterol 12 mg, Sodium 82 mg, Carbs 23.9 g (Fiber 2.3 g, Sugars 11.3 g), Protein 3.4 g

BAR TIPS

—Even though almost all of the quinoa available in the U.S. comes pre-rinsed (meaning the naturally occurring bitter coating called saponin has been removed), you should still rinse your quinoa before cooking. Why? Because trace amounts of saponin residue may remain during processing, leading to a bitter taste. Rinsing the quinoa is no chore: simply place the quinoa in a fine-mesh strainer and rinse thoroughly under cold water for 30 to 60 seconds.

—Be sure to use very ripe bananas for this recipe; the skins should be mostly brown. It will take approximately three to four medium-large, very ripe bananas to equal 1 1/2 cups mashed bananas.

—You can substitute 1 cup of your favorite cooked cooled grain—e.g., bulgur, buckwheat, brown rice—for the cooked, cooled quinoa (a great way to use up leftovers!).

BAR KEEPING

Tightly wrap the bars individually in plastic wrap.

REFRIGERATOR: 1 week
FREEZER: 3 months in airtight container; thaw 1 hour

BAR VARIATIONS

MAPLE-BLUEBERRY BANANA BARS
Use maple syrup for the sweetener. Use an equal amount of dried blueberries in place of the dried cherries and 1 teaspoon pure maple extract in place of the vanilla.

TROPICAL BANANA BARS
Use an equal amount of ground allspice in place of the cinnamon, an equal amout of dried tropical fruit bits or chopped dried mango in place of the dried cherries, and an equal amout of unsweetened flaked or shredded coconut in place of the walnuts. Omit the chocolate chips.

PEANUT-CHOCOLATE BANANA BARS
Omit the cinnamon and dried cherries and use 2/3 cup dry, roasted peanuts (unsalted or lightly salted) in place of the walnuts.

BANANA MUESLI BARS
Use an equal amount of pepitas or sunflower seeds in place of walnuts and 1/3 cup flake or shredded coconut in place of the chocolate chips. If desired, spread or drizzle cooled bars with Greek Yogurt Bar Coating (see page 31).

ENDURANCE
BARS

Sporting a perfect balance of complex carbohydrates and protein, endurance bars are ideal before—or in the midst of—extensive stretches of continuous activity, such as long workouts, long work days, running after a toddler, or keeping up with a new (and hyper) puppy. The complex carbohydrates in these bars are essential fuel that the body can convert into glucose to provide you with a great source of energy. Adding protein and healthy fats to the mix helps slow the rate that the body absorbs those carbohydrates, thereby extending your energy supply for longer periods. I've figured out the ratios for you in each delicious bar; all you need to remember is a big bottle of water for accompaniment.

CHICKPEA CHAMPION BARS

2 cups old-fashioned or quick-cooking rolled oats

1 1/4 cups nuts, seeds, or a combination

1 cup dried fruit, chopped (e.g., apricots, apples, cherries, raisins)

3 tablespoons flaxseed meal

1/2 cup nondairy milk or low-fat milk, warmed

1 cup canned, no-sodium chickpeas, rinsed and drained

1/2 cup natural, unsweetened nut or seed butter (e.g., peanut, cashew, or sunflower)

1/2 cup packed pitted, soft dates

1/4 cup agave nectar, honey, or pure maple syrup

1 teaspoon ground cinnamon

1/4 tsp fine sea salt

As much as I love falafel, hummus, and chickpea burgers, this is one of my favorite ways to eat my favorite bean. Dense, filling, and chewy, they will make you the hero of your running group. And if you are wondering what chickpeas taste like in a power bar, the answer is nothing because you won't know they are there at all. What you will think is oatmeal cookie meets peanut butter blondie, punctuated by plenty of seeds, nuts, and dried fruit. The options for variation are vast, so happy experimenting! **MAKES 20 BARS**

1. Line a 9 by 13-inch baking pan with foil or parchment paper and spray with nonstick cooking spray.

2. Preheat oven to 350°F.

3. Spread the oats and the nuts or seeds on a large rimmed baking sheet. Bake in the preheated oven for 6 to 8 minutes, shaking halfway through, until golden and fragrant; transfer to the bowl of a food processor and let cool.

4. Process the oats mixture, using on/off pulses, until the nuts and seeds are coarsely chopped; transfer to a large bowl. Mix in the dried fruit.

5. Meanwhile, combine the flaxseed meal and warm milk in a small bowl until blended. Let stand for 5 minutes before using.

6. Place the chickpeas, nut or seed butter, dates, agave nectar, cinnamon, salt, and flax mixture in the food processor (no need to clean bowl); process until the mixture is smooth.

7. Add the chickpea mixture to the oats mixture, mixing with a spatula until coated.

8. Transfer the mixture to the prepared pan. Place a large piece of parchment paper, wax paper, or plastic wrap (coated with nonstick cooking spray) atop the bar mixture and use it to spread and flatten the mixture evenly in the pan. Discard the paper or plastic.

Nutrients per bar: Calories 221, Fat 10.7 g, (Saturated 2.3 g), Cholesterol 0 mg, Sodium 38 mg, Carbs 26.3 g (Fiber 4.7 g, Sugars 12.3 g), Protein 7.7 g

9. Bake in the preheated oven for 15 to 18 minutes or until the edges are golden brown and the top appears somewhat dry. Transfer to a wire rack and cool completely.

10. Using the liner, lift the mixture from the pan and transfer to a cutting board. Cut into 20 bars.

BAR TIPS

—You can swap an equal amount of canned white beans or pinto beans for the chickpeas.

—You can use an equal amount of chia seeds in place of the flaxseed meal.

—There's no need to limit yourself to oats for the whole grain flakes; try an equal amount of quinoa, spelt, kamut, or rice flakes in their place.

BAR KEEPING

Tightly wrap the bars individually in plastic wrap.

ROOM TEMP: 2 days
REFRIGERATOR: 1 week
FREEZER: 3 months in airtight container; thaw 1 hour

BAR VARIATIONS

CHOCOLATE CHIP CHICKPEA BLONDIES
Replace the dried fruit with 1/2 cup miniature semisweet chocolate chips. Use an equal amount of dark (cooking) molasses in place of the agave nectar and replace the cinnamon with 2 teaspoons vanilla extract.

DOUBLE CHOCOLATE BLACK BEAN BARS
Replace the dried fruit with 1/2 cup miniature semisweet chocolate chips and replace the flaxseed meal with 1/4 cup unsweetened, natural cocoa powder (not Dutch process). Replace the cinnamon with 2 teaspoons vanilla extract.

TOASTED COCONUT CANNELLINI BARS
Replace the chickpeas with an equal amount of cannellini beans (or other white beans). Omit the dried fruit and toast 1 cup unsweetened flake or shredded coconut along with the oats and nuts. Replace the cinnamon with 1 teaspoon vanilla extract.

GREEK YOGURT MUESLI BARS

1 1/2 cups old-fashioned or quick-cooking rolled oats

1/2 cup nuts, chopped (e.g., almonds, cashews, walnuts, pistachios)

1/4 cup seeds (e.g., sesame seeds, sunflower seeds, hemp hearts)

1/4 cup unsweetened flake or shredded coconut, finely chopped

1/2 cup lightly packed all-natural, sweetened vanilla whey protein powder

1 large egg

2/3 cup plain nonfat Greek yogurt

1/3 cup natural, unsweetened nut or seed butter (e.g., peanut, cashew, or sunflower)

3 tablespoons honey or agave nectar

2 tablespoons virgin coconut oil, warmed until melted, or vegetable oil

1 tablespoon finely grated lemon or orange zest

1/2 cup chopped dried fruit (e.g., cherries, apricots, figs, raisins)

Greek Yogurt Bar Coating (optional; see page 31)

Few people have survived on a tiny tropical island by eating muesli, but I am one such person. To make a long story short, there was a dreadful "resort" that featured two breakfast items: leaden German pancakes and muesli. Lunch was not served at all, and with no stores on the island, I would down 3 bowls of muesli every morning. This could turn many off muesli forevermore, but it did the reverse for me: give me a lumpy-bumpy bowl of yogurt, oats, seeds, and fruit any morning and I am a happy camper. Here I've created a portable version of my favorite mélange. **MAKES 12 BARS**

1. Line an 8-inch square baking pan with foil or parchment paper and spray with nonstick cooking spray.

2. Preheat oven to 350°F.

3. Spread the oats, nuts, seeds, and coconut on a large rimmed baking sheet. Bake in the preheated oven for 6 to 8 minutes, shaking halfway through, until golden and fragrant. Transfer to a large bowl and let cool; stir in the protein powder.

4. Mix together the egg, yogurt, nut or seed butter, honey, oil, and lemon zest until blended.

5. Add the yogurt mixture to the oats mixture and stir until just blended. Mix in the dried fruit.

6. Spread the batter evenly in the prepared pan.

7. Bake in the preheated oven for 13 to 16 minutes or until top is golden brown and a toothpick inserted in the center comes out clean. Transfer to a wire rack and cool completely. Spread or drizzle the mixture with the bar coating, if using; refrigerate for 30 minutes.

8. Using the liner, lift the mixture from the pan and transfer to a cutting board. Cut into 12 bars.

BAR TIPS

—If you don't want to use protein powder, simply increase the total amount of oats by 1/3 cup. Alternatively, add 1/4 cup of flaxseed meal or 1/2 cup of nonfat instant milk powder.

—Be sure to use Greek yogurt for the recipe. It is a strained yogurt, which means it has a much lower water content than regular yogurt.

—If you'd like to use regular dairy or nondairy yogurt, strain 2 cups of it through a cheesecloth or coffee filter overnight. Discard the excess liquid and use 2/3 cup of the strained yogurt.

Nutrients per bar: Calories 214, Fat 11.5 g, (Saturated 2.6 g), Cholesterol 9 mg, Sodium 79 mg, Carbs 19.8 g (Fiber 2.1 g, Sugars 9.5 g), Protein 10.2 g

BAR KEEPING

Tightly wrap the bars individually in plastic wrap.

ROOM TEMP: 3 days
REFRIGERATOR: 1 week
FREEZER: 3 months in airtight container; thaw 1 hour

BAR VARIATIONS

QUINOA, KAMUT, OR SPELT MUESLI BARS
Replace the oats with an equal amount of quinoa, kamut, or spelt flakes.

VEGAN YOGURT MUESLI BARS
Use strained nondairy yogurt (see tip) in place of the Greek yogurt, agave nectar in place of the honey, and vegan protein powder in place of whey. Use 1 tablespoon flaxseed meal, mixed with 3 tablespoons warm water, in place of the egg.

PUMPKIN PIE POWER BARS

3/4 cup quick-cooking or old-fashioned rolled oats

1 1/4 cup pumpkin purée (not pie filling)

1 cup lightly packed all-natural, sweetened vanilla whey protein powder

1/4 cup dark (cooking) molasses, pure maple syrup, or honey

1/2 cup plain nonfat Greek yogurt

2 large eggs

1 tablespoon pumpkin pie spice

2 teaspoons vanilla extract

1 teaspoon baking powder

1/4 teaspoon fine sea salt

Dark Chocolate Bar Coating or Greek Yogurt Bar Coating (optional; see page 31)

Pumpkin has a wealth of powerful antioxidants known as carotenoids, organic pigments that have the potential to ward off various types of cancer and heart disease, along with cataracts and macular degeneration. But what else can pumpkin do for power bars? How about add richness, deep flavor, and moisture, with a minimum of calories and no fat. If you want to up the pumpkin ante further, sprinkle the bars with pepitas (green pumpkin seeds). They add great crunch, color, and nutty flavor, as well as protein. MAKES 10 BARS

1. Line an 8-inch square baking pan with foil or parchment paper and spray with nonstick cooking spray.

2. Preheat oven to 350°F.

3. Process the oats in a food processor until they resemble a fine powder.

4. Add all of the remaining ingredients (except the bar coating) and process until completely blended.

5. Spread the batter evenly in the prepared pan.

6. Bake in the preheated oven for 25 to 28 minutes or until the edges are beginning to brown and a toothpick inserted in the center comes out clean. Transfer to a wire rack and cool completely. Spread or drizzle the mixture with the bar coating, if using; refrigerate for 30 minutes.

7. Using the liner, lift the mixture from the pan and transfer to a cutting board. Cut into 10 bars. Store in the refrigerator or freezer.

Nutrients per bar: Calories 127, Fat 2.3 g, (Saturated 0.8 g), Cholesterol 58 mg, Sodium 130 mg, Carbs 15 g (Fiber 1.5 g, Sugars 7.2 g), Protein 12 g

BAR TIP

—No pumpkin pie spice? No problem. You can make your own by combining 1 1/2 teaspoons ground cinnamon, 1 teaspoon ground ginger, 1/4 teaspoon ground nutmeg, and 1/4 teaspoon ground cloves to replace the 1 tablespoon of pumpkin pie spice.

BAR KEEPING

Tightly wrap the bars individually in plastic wrap.

REFRIGERATOR: 1 week
FREEZER: 3 months in airtight container; thaw 1 hour

BAR VARIATIONS

SUGAR-FREE PUMPKIN POWER BARS
Replace the molasses with 1 teaspoon liquid stevia. Increase yogurt to 2/3 cup.

PUMPKIN LATTE POWER BARS
Add 1 tablespoon instant espresso powder, dissolved in 1 tablespoon warm water, to the remaining ingredients in the food processor before blending.

PUMPKIN CRANBERRY BARS
Add 2/3 cup dried cranberries and 1 tablespoon finely grated orange zest to the remaining ingredients in the food processor before blending.

EXTRA FANCY PUMPKIN BARS
Prepare as directed. Before cutting, spread the top of the bars with Dark Chocolate Bar Coating (see page 31) and sprinkle with 1/2 cup toasted pepitas (green pumpkin seeds).

CHOCOLATE CHIP PUMPKIN BARS
Add 1/3 cup miniature semisweet chocolate chips to the batter.

FLAX YOUR MUSCLES BARS

1 1/4 cups flaxseed meal

1 1/4 cups quick-cooking rolled oats

1 cup roasted, lightly salted sunflower seeds

1 cup dried fruit, chopped (e.g., apricots, dates, cherries)

1/2 cup cacao nibs

2/3 cup honey, agave syrup, or pure maple syrup

2/3 cup natural, unsweetened nut or seed butter (e.g., peanut, cashew, or sunflower)

1/4 cup water

1 teaspoon vanilla extract

Flaxseeds have a superiority complex: they are one of the world's healthiest foods, rich in omega-3 fatty acids (ahem…make that the best plant source of omega-3 fatty acids), high in fiber (both soluble and insoluble), a significant source of protein, and loaded with lignans, a type of phytoestrogen that may protect against certain types of cancer. All you need to know in the case of these bars, though, is that they have a nutty, toasty, simply terrific flavor. MAKES 16 BARS

1. Line a 9-inch square baking pan with foil or parchment paper and spray with nonstick cooking spray.

2. Place the flaxseed meal, oats, seeds, dried fruit, and cacao nibs in a food processor.

3. Meanwhile, combine the honey, nut or seed butter, and water in a small saucepan. Heat over medium-low, stirring, for 4 to 5 minutes until the mixture is melted and slightly bubbly. Remove from heat and stir in vanilla.

4. Immediately pour the honey mixture over the flaxseed meal mixture in the food processor. Process, using on/off pulses, until the mixture is finely chopped and begins to clump together.

5. Transfer the mixture to the prepared pan. Place a large piece of parchment paper, wax paper, or plastic wrap (coated with nonstick cooking spray) atop the bar mixture and use it to spread, flatten, and very firmly compact the mixture evenly in the pan. Cool at least 1 hour until firmly set.

6. Using the liner, lift the mixture from the pan and transfer to a cutting board. Cut into 16 bars.

Nutrients per bar: Calories 252, Fat 12.4 g, (Saturated 2.4 g), Cholesterol 0 mg, Sodium 27 mg, Carbs 26.4 g (Fiber 7.1 g, Sugars 17.8 g), Protein 8.9 g

BAR TIPS

—If you do not have cacao nibs, simply increase the total amount of sunflower seeds to 1 1/4 cups and add 1 tablespoon natural unsweetened cocoa powder.

—Roasted sunflower seeds add tremendous flavor to these bars, but you can use raw seeds too. Alternatively, toast raw sunflower seeds in a large dry skillet over medium heat for 3 to 4 minutes until golden and fragrant.

—If the bar mixture seems too dry after processing, add a bit more water, 1 teaspoon at a time, until it just begins to clump together.

BAR KEEPING

Tightly wrap the bars individually in plastic wrap.

ROOM TEMP: 2 days
REFRIGERATOR: 2 weeks
FREEZER: 3 months in airtight container; thaw 1 hour

BAR VARIATIONS

BANANA-BLUEBERRY FLAX BARS
Replace the cacao nibs with 1/2 cup crushed banana chips and use dried blueberries for the dried fruit.

TROPICAL FRUIT FLAX BARS
Replace the cacao nibs with 1/2 cup unsweetened flake or shredded coconut and use chopped tropical fruit bits for the dried fruit. Add 1 teaspoon ground allspice along with the vanilla.

TOASTED WALNUT-RAISIN FLAX BARS
Omit the cacao nibs and replace the sunflower seeds with 1 1/2 cups toasted walnuts, chopped. Use raisins for the dried fruit and add 1 teaspoon ground cinnamon along with the vanilla.

FIG & HONEY LENTIL
GRANOLA BARS

1/2 cup dried red lentils

1 1/2 cups water

1 tablespoon virgin coconut oil or vegetable oil

1 3/4 cups quinoa flakes or quick-cooking rolled oats

1/2 cup toasted nuts or seeds, chopped (e.g., almonds, pecans, sunflower seeds, pepitas)

1/2 cup natural, unsweetened nut or seed butter (e.g., peanut, cashew, or sunflower)

2/3 cup dried figs, chopped

1 tablespoon honey

1 teaspoon vanilla extract

1/2 teaspoon fine sea salt

1/2 teaspoon ground cardamom

Lentils? In a granola bar? Yes and yes! Red lentils become super soft and mushy once cooked; once mashed further, they work in tandem with the nut or seed butter to hold the bars together and lend hours of staying power. Besides being cheap and easy-to-prepare (no soaking required!), lentils boast high levels of protein, folic acid, dietary fiber, vitamin C, B vitamins, essential amino acids, and trace minerals. Have fun serving them to friends, family, and fitness buddies; they will never guess the secret ingredient. **MAKES 12 BARS**

1. Line an 8-inch square baking pan with foil or parchment paper and spray with nonstick cooking spray.

2. Place the lentils in a fine mesh strainer and rinse thoroughly in cold running water. Transfer to a medium saucepan and add the 1 1/2 cups water. Bring to a boil over medium-high heat, then cover and simmer for 18 to 22 minutes or until the water has absorbed and the lentils are cooked through; transfer to a large bowl.

3. Mash the lentils with the tines of a fork (they should already be soft, which is typical with red lentils). Let cool 5 minutes.

4. Meanwhile, melt the coconut oil in a large skillet over medium heat. Add the quinoa flakes and nuts or seeds. Cook, stirring frequently, for 3 to 4 minutes or until the flakes and nuts or seeds are golden and fragrant.

5. Add the quinoa flake mixture, nut or seed butter, dried figs, honey, vanilla, salt, and cardamom to the lentils, mixing with a spatula until coated.

6. Transfer the mixture to the prepared pan. Place a large piece of parchment paper, wax paper, or plastic wrap (coated with nonstick cooking spray) atop the bar mixture and use it to spread, flatten, and very firmly compact the mixture evenly in the pan. Refrigerate at least 2 hours until firmly set.

7. Using the liner, lift the mixture from the pan and transfer to a cutting board. Cut into 12 bars. Store in the refrigerator or freezer.

Nutrients per bar: Calories 226, Fat 10.2 g, (Saturated 1.7 g), Cholesterol 0 mg, Sodium 102 mg, Carbs 25.8 g (Fiber 4.9 g, Sugars 8.2 g), Protein 9.1 g

BAR TIPS

—If red lentils are unavailable, regular brown lentils may be substituted. Use an equal amount of brown lentils, but increase the total amount of water to 1 3/4 cups. Cook the lentils for approximately 7 to 9 minutes longer or until the water is absorbed and the lentils are cooked through and very soft.

—Other dried fruits (such as raisins, cherries, and apricots) may be used in place of the dried figs.

—An equal amount of agave nectar, maple syrup, brown rice syrup, or DIY Glucose Syrup (see page 30) may be used in place of the honey.

BAR KEEPING

Tightly wrap the bars individually in plastic wrap.

REFRIGERATOR: 1 week
FREEZER: 3 months in airtight container; thaw 1 hour

BAR VARIATIONS

CRANBERRY-PECAN LENTIL BARS
Use maple syrup in place of the honey, toasted pecans for the nuts, and dried cranberries in place of the figs.

TAHINI-LEMON LENTIL BARS
Use toasted walnuts for the nuts, tahini for the seed butter, and dates in place of the figs. Replace the vanilla extract with 1 tablespoon finely grated lemon zest and 2 teaspoons fresh lemon juice.

QUINOA CHIA APRICOT BARS

3/4 cup packed pitted, soft dates

2/3 cup unsweetened apple juice

1/3 cup chia seeds

1 tablespoon vanilla extract

2 tablespoons virgin coconut oil or vegetable oil

1 1/2 cups quinoa flakes

1 cup walnuts, chopped

1/2 cup sesame seeds

3/4 teaspoon ground cardamom or ground ginger

3/4 teaspoon ground cinnamon

1/4 teaspoon fine sea salt

1 1/2 cups dried apricots, coarsely chopped

A cinch to prepare, these power bars are built on a foundation of two superfood seeds: chia and quinoa. Both are rich sources of fiber, protein, and omega-3 fatty acids, as well as vitamins and minerals. They are guaranteed to put a smile on all of your friends' and family's faces, even the ones who insist they don't like "healthy" food and especially if you have whipped up a batch of kale smoothies as accompaniment. **MAKES 16 BARS**

1. Line a 9-inch square baking pan with foil or parchment paper and spray with nonstick cooking spray.

2. Preheat oven to 350°F.

3. Combine the dates and apple juice in a blender. Let stand for 10 minutes and then blend until smooth. Add the chia seeds and vanilla extract to the blender; pulse two or three times to blend. Let stand 10 minutes to allow the chia seeds to gel.

4. Meanwhile, melt the coconut oil in a large skillet over medium heat. Add the quinoa flakes, walnuts, and sesame seeds. Cook, stirring frequently, for 3 to 4 minutes or until the flakes, nuts, and seeds are golden and fragrant. Add the cardamom, cinnamon, and salt to the skillet; cook and stir for 30 seconds longer. Transfer to a large bowl.

5. Add the date mixture and apricots to the quinoa flake mixture, mixing with a spatula until combined.

6. Transfer the mixture to the prepared pan. Place a large piece of parchment paper, wax paper, or plastic wrap (coated with nonstick cooking spray) atop the bar mixture and use it to spread, flatten, and very firmly compact the mixture evenly in the pan. Discard the paper or plastic.

Nutrients per bar: Calories 183, Fat 9.4 g, (Saturated 2.1 g), Cholesterol 0 mg, Sodium 38 mg, Carbs 22.7 g (Fiber 2.9 g, Sugars 12 g), Protein 4.5 g

7. Bake in the preheated oven for 20 to 25 minutes or until the edges are golden brown and the top of the bars appears somewhat dry. Transfer to a wire rack and cool completely.

8. Using the liner, lift the mixture from the pan and transfer to a cutting board. Cut into 16 bars.

BAR TIP

—This is my preferred blend of nuts, seeds, and dried fruit, but you can vary them as much as you like according to your taste and what you have on hand.

BAR KEEPING

Tightly wrap the bars individually in plastic wrap.

ROOM TEMP: 2 days
REFRIGERATOR: 1 week
FREEZER: 3 months in airtight container; thaw 1 hour

BAR VARIATION

BETTER-THAN-A-BOWL-OF-OATMEAL BARS
Replace the quinoa flakes with an equal amount of quick-cooking rolled oats and replace the dried apricots with 3/4 cup dried cherries (or cranberries) and 3/4 cup dried blueberries.

QUINOA CHIA
APRICOT BARS

RECIPE
PAGE
90

SEEDS
OF POWER
BARS

RECIPE
PAGE
94

PEPITA &
POPPED
AMARANTH
BARS

RECIPE
PAGE
96

SEEDS OF POWER BARS

1 1/2 cups quinoa flakes or quick-cooking rolled oats

1/4 cup sesame seeds

1/4 cup millet or hemp hearts

1/4 cup chia seeds or poppy seeds

1/4 cup flaxseed meal

3/4 cup plain nondairy milk or low-fat dairy milk

3/4 cup uncooked multigrain hot cereal

3/4 cup natural, unsweetened sunflower seed butter or tahini

1/2 cup agave nectar or honey

1 tablespoon finely grated orange or lemon zest

1/4 teaspoon fine sea salt

1 cup dried cherries or dried cranberries, roughly chopped

Who knew that sowing the seeds of power was as simple as whipping up a batch of no-bake power bars? Ok, I did. Seeds really are packed with power—think of any seed as a concentrated dose of vitamins, minerals, fiber, and essential fatty acids. They are a perfect alternative to nuts, but these bars demonstrate that they are far more than understudies. One of these bars and a big bottle of water are all you need for your next power trek whether across town or country. **MAKES 20 BARS**

1. Line a 9-inch square baking pan with foil or parchment paper and spray with nonstick cooking spray.

2. Preheat oven to 350°F.

3. Spread the quinoa flakes, sesame seeds, and millet on a large rimmed baking sheet. Bake in the preheated oven for 6 to 8 minutes, shaking halfway through, until golden and fragrant. Transfer to a large bowl; stir in the chia seeds and flaxseed meal.

4. Bring the milk to a boil in a small saucepan set over medium heat. Remove the pan from the heat and stir in the cereal; cover and let stand for 2 minutes. Add the sunflower seed butter, agave nectar, orange zest, and salt. Cook and stir the mixture over low heat for 7 minutes, until thickened and all of the liquid is absorbed.

5. Immediately add the cereal mixture and the cherries to the quinoa mixture, mixing with a spatula until coated.

6. Transfer the mixture to the prepared pan. Place a large piece of parchment paper, wax paper, or plastic wrap (coated with nonstick cooking spray) atop the bar mixture and use it to spread, flatten, and very firmly compact the mixture evenly in the pan. Refrigerate at least 2 hours until firmly set.

7. Using the liner, lift the mixture from the pan and transfer to a cutting board. Cut into 20 bars.

Nutrients per bar: Calories 199, Fat 9.2 g, (Saturated 3 g), Cholesterol 0 mg, Sodium 37 mg, Carbs 24.8 g (Fiber 3.3 g, Sugars 12.6 g), Protein 6.1 g

BAR TIPS

—Seeds of all varieties can become rancid quickly due to their high oil content. To keep them fresh as long as possible, store them in an airtight container in the refrigerator or freezer.

—Vary the type and amounts of the different seeds as much as you like so long as the total amount equals 3/4 cup.

BAR KEEPING

Tightly wrap the bars individually in plastic wrap.

ROOM TEMP: 2 days
REFRIGERATOR: 1 week
FREEZER: 3 months in airtight container; thaw 1 hour

BAR VARIATIONS

SESAME CASHEW BARS
Prepare as directed, but replace the millet and chia seeds with 1/2 cup finely chopped raw cashews and replace the sunflower seed butter with an equal amount of natural, unsweetened cashew butter. Replace the orange zest with 2 teaspoons vanilla extract and add 1 1/2 teaspoons ground ginger along with the salt.

SUNFLOWER-FIG BARS
Prepare as directed, but replace the sesame seeds, millet, and chia seeds with 3/4 cup raw sunflower seeds. Use lemon zest, not orange zest.

PEPITA & POPPED AMARANTH BARS (DULCE DE ALEGRÍA)

1/3 cup pepitas (green pumpkin seeds)

3 tablespoons packed dried unsweetened mango or pineapple, finely chopped

3 tablespoons packed dried cranberries or dried cherries, finely chopped

2/3 cup uncooked amaranth

6 tablespoons honey

2 tablespoons natural cane sugar

3 tablespoons virgin coconut oil or unsalted butter

1/4 teaspoon fine sea salt

1 tablespoon finely grated lime zest

Dulce de alegría are sweet, light and crispy Mexican bars reminiscent of crispy rice treats, but with a super-healthy twist: amaranth, one of the most nutritious foods in the world (make that universe), is popped in a hot pan to take the place of crisp rice cereal. Natural sweeteners (not artificially-flavored marshmallows) hold everything together in sweet harmony. Amaranth is technically a pseudo-cereal (not a grain, much like quinoa), and was grown for centuries by the Aztecs. It has twice as much iron as wheat, is high in protein and fiber, and has a mild, sweet, nutty, and subtly malt-like flavor. Popping the seeds takes a few minutes, as you can only pop a tablespoon at a time, but the result looks like the world's teeniest, tiniest popcorn—what's not to love about that? If you are still not convinced, consider this: the literal translation of alegría is happiness, which is exactly what you will experience when you take a bite. MAKES 10 BARS

1. Line an 8-inch square baking pan with foil or parchment paper and spray with nonstick cooking spray.

2. Heat a deep dry saucepan or stockpot over medium-high heat. Add the pepitas and toast, gently shaking pan, until they begin to make a popping sound, turn golden at the edges, and smell fragrant, about 1 to 2 minutes. Transfer to a cutting board and cool slightly. Coarsely chop the pepitas; transfer to a large bowl. Mix in the dried mango and cranberries.

3. Reheat the pan over high heat until very hot. To test if pan is hot enough, add a drop of water to the pan; it should turn into a bead and dance across the pan. Add 1 tablespoon of the amaranth. Vigorously shake the pan or stir with a wooden spoon until the seeds pop, about 12 to 18 seconds (watch closely as the seeds will burn quickly when the popping is finished). Immediately transfer the popped seeds to the bowl with the pepita mixture. Continue popping the remaining amaranth, 1 tablespoon at a time, in the same fashion. (You should yield about 2 1/2 cups of popped amaranth.)

Nutrients per bar: Calories 170, Fat 6.8 g, (Saturated 4.1 g), Cholesterol 0 mg, Sodium 63 mg, Carbs 26.5 g (Fiber 1.6 g, Sugars 16.3 g), Protein 3.1 g

4. Combine the honey, sugar, oil, and salt in a small saucepan. Cook, stirring constantly, over medium heat for 2 to 3 minutes or until the sugar is melted and the mixture bubbles and begins to turn golden brown.

5. Immediately stir in the lime zest and then pour the mixture over the amaranth mixture, mixing with a spatula until coated.

6. Transfer the mixture to the prepared pan. Place a large piece of parchment paper, wax paper, or plastic wrap (coated with nonstick cooking spray) atop the bar mixture and use it to spread, flatten, and compact the mixture evenly in the pan. Cool completely.

7. Using the liner, lift the mixture from the pan and transfer to a cutting board. Cut into 10 bars.

BAR TIPS

—Just like old popcorn, old amaranth will not pop well. For best results, check the expiration date on the package and use before the date has passed.

—Be forewarned: some of the amaranth will pop right out of the pan, so be sure to use your deepest pan or pot.

BAR KEEPING

Tightly wrap the bars individually in plastic wrap.

ROOM TEMP: 3 days
REFRIGERATOR: 2 weeks
FREEZER: 3 months in airtight container; thaw 1/2 hour

BAR VARIATIONS

CINNAMON-CASHEW AMARANTH BARS
Replace the pepitas, dried mango, and dried cranberries with 1 cup roasted, lightly salted cashews, chopped. Omit the lime zest and add 1 teaspoon vanilla extract and 1 teaspoon ground cinnamon to the warm syrup mixture.

SPICY PEANUT AMARANTH BARS
Replace the pepitas, dried mango, and dried cranberries with 1 cup roasted, lightly salted peanuts, chopped. Add 1/4 teaspoon cayenne pepper along with the lime zest.

MEGA MARATHON BARS

1/2 cup quick-cooking rolled oats

1/2 cup nuts or seeds (e.g., walnuts, almonds, pepitas, sunflower seeds)

3/4 cup dried fruit (e.g., blueberries, apricots, cherries, raisins)

2/3 cup white whole-wheat flour or whole wheat pastry flour

1/3 cup lightly packed all-natural, sweetened vanilla whey protein powder

2 tablespoons flaxseed meal

3/4 teaspoon baking powder

1/4 teaspoon baking soda

1/4 teaspoon fine sea salt

1 large egg

1/2 cup low-fat milk

1/4 cup honey, agave nectar, or pure maple syrup

2 tablespoons virgin coconut oil, warmed until melted, or vegetable oil

3/4 teaspoon almond extract

Although these gently sweet stunners make a great race-day power snack, they are also perfect for making at the drop of a hat for any group (wee ones, book clubs, knitting circles, Ultimate Frisbee), on any occasion. Let's face it, we all need stamina for our myriad activities, and these bars, with their healthy balance of complex carbohydrates, healthy fats, and protein, provide it. Deliciously.
MAKES 9 BARS

1. Line an 8-inch square baking pan with foil or parchment paper and spray with nonstick cooking spray.

2. Preheat oven to 325°F.

3. Spread the oats and nuts on a large rimmed baking sheet. Bake in the preheated oven for 6 to 8 minutes, shaking halfway through, until golden and fragrant. Transfer to a food processor and cool 5 minutes.

4. Add the dried fruit to the oats mixture. Process, using on/off pulses, until coarsely chopped; transfer to a large bowl.

5. Add the flour, protein powder, flaxseed meal, baking powder, baking soda, and salt to the oats mixture.

6. Whisk the egg, milk, honey, oil, and almond extract in a small bowl until blended.

7. Add the egg mixture to the oats mixture, mixing until well blended.

8. Spread the batter evenly in the prepared pan.

9. Bake in the preheated oven for 23 to 28 minutes or until the edges are beginning to brown and a toothpick inserted in the center comes out clean. Transfer to a wire rack and cool completely.

10. Using the liner, lift the mixture from the pan and transfer to a cutting board. Cut into 9 bars.

Nutrients per bar: Calories 192, Fat 6.1 g, (Saturated 3.1 g), Cholesterol 27 mg, Sodium 98 mg, Carbs 29.2 g (Fiber 2 g, Sugars 16.2 g), Protein 6.8 g

BAR KEEPING

Tightly wrap the bars individually in plastic wrap.

ROOM TEMP: 2 days
REFRIGERATOR: 1 week
FREEZER: 3 months in airtight container; thaw 1 hour

BAR VARIATIONS

CHUNKY CHERRY MARATHON BARS
Use walnuts or pecans for the nuts and dried cherries for the dried fruit. Sprinkle the batter with 1/3 cup miniature semisweet chocolate chips before baking.

RAISIN MOLASSES MARATHON BARS
Use walnuts or pecans for the nuts, raisins for the dried fruit, and an equal amount of dark (cooking) molasses in place of the honey. Replace the almond extract with 1 teaspoon vanilla extract.

GLUTEN-FREE MARATHON BARS
Use an equal amount of your favorite all-purpose, gluten-free flour blend in place of the white whole-wheat flour.

MANGO MARATHON BARS
Replace the nuts with an equal amount of dried unsweetened flake or shredded coconut and use dried mango for the fruit.

VEGAN MARATHON BARS
To make these bars vegan, replace the whey protein powder with an equal amount of all-natural, sweetened vanilla vegan protein powder and opt for plain nondairy milk. Replace the egg with a flaxseed or chia "egg": combine 1 tablespoon flaxseed meal or chia seeds with 3 tablespoons warm water, then let stand 5 minutes to thicken. Use agave nectar or maple syrup instead of the honey.

TOASTED WHEAT GERM BARS

1 cup packed pitted, soft dates

1 cup warm water

1 cup pecans, toasted or raw

1/2 cup low-fat milk or plain nondairy milk

1/4 cup pure maple syrup, honey, or agave nectar

2 large eggs

3 tablespoons vegetable oil or virgin coconut oil

1 teaspoon ground cinnamon

1 teaspoon baking powder

1/4 teaspoon fine sea salt

1 3/4 cups toasted wheat germ

1/2 cup lightly packed all-natural, sweetened vanilla whey protein powder

Wheat germ—the vitamin- and mineral-rich embryo of the wheat kernel—was a health food superstar in the 1970s, enriching yogurt, granola, casseroles, and funky salads with equal ease. But this tiny ingredient is no one-shot wonder—it continues to rock on in the new millennium. Why? Because it is a superfood if ever there was one. Consider this: two tablespoons of wheat germ has about 1.5 grams of unsaturated fat, 9 grams of complex carbohydrates, 4 grams of protein, 2 grams of dietary fiber, 2 grams of sugars, no cholesterol, and a mere 60 calories. Add to that a slew of vitamins and minerals including B vitamins (such as folate, niacin, thiamin, and vitamin B6), calcium, iron, magnesium, manganese, omega-3 fatty acids, phosphorous, potassium, selenium, vitamin E, and zinc. Go germs! Most importantly, wheat germ is readily available, affordable, and makes a simply smashing power bar that will help you endure the most wicked workout or summit the largest mountain of laundry. **MAKES 16 BARS**

1. Line a 9-inch square baking pan with foil or parchment paper and spray with nonstick cooking spray.

2. Preheat oven to 350°F.

3. Combine the dates and warm water in a small bowl. Let stand for 5 to 10 minutes until fruit is soft (time will vary according to the dryness of the dates). Drain and pat dry with paper towels.

4. Meanwhile, place the pecans in a food processor and process until finely chopped (but not a paste). Add the drained dates. Process, using on/off pulses, until the dates are finely chopped and blended and the mixture begins to stick together and clump on the sides of the bowl.

5. Add the milk, maple syrup, eggs, oil, cinnamon, baking powder, and salt to the food processor bowl; process until blended. Transfer mixture to a large bowl.

6. Add the wheat germ and protein powder to the date mixture, stirring until well blended.

Nutrients per bar: Calories 203, Fat 11.4 g, (Saturated 3.1 g), Cholesterol 29 mg, Sodium 60 mg, Carbs 20.4 g (Fiber 3.5 g, Sugars 13 g), Protein 8 g

7. Spread batter evenly in the prepared pan.

8. Bake in the preheated oven for 33 to 38 minutes or until set in the center. Transfer to a wire rack and cool completely.

9. Using the liner, lift the mixture from the pan and transfer to a cutting board. Cut into 16 bars.

BAR TIPS

—You can either use pre-toasted wheat germ (more commonly available in grocery stores) or toast raw wheat germ yourself: spread wheat germ on a large rimmed baking sheet and bake in a 350°F oven for 5 to 8 minutes, stirring once, until golden and fragrant. Let cool completely before using.

—An equal amount of other nuts (e.g., walnuts, cashews, peanuts) or sunflower seeds may be used in place of the pecans.

—Consider adding up to 1/3 cup chopped dried fruit, miniature semisweet chocolate chips, or cacao nibs along with the wheat germ.

—Consider coating or drizzling the bars with any of the bar coatings on page 31.

BAR KEEPING

Tightly wrap the bars individually in plastic wrap.

ROOM TEMP: 2 days
REFRIGERATOR: 1 week
FREEZER: 3 months in airtight container; thaw 1 hour

BAR VARIATIONS

APRICOT-AGAVE WHEAT GERM BARS
Use an equal amount of dried apricots in place of the dates and use agave nectar for the sweetener. Replace the cinnamon with an equal amount of ground ginger.

GLUTEN-FREE FLAX BARS
Prepare as directed but use an equal amount of flaxseed meal in place of the toasted wheat germ.

CHOCOLATE WHEAT GERM BARS
Use an equal amount of chocolate protein powder in place of the vanilla protein powder. Reduce the wheat germ to 1 1/2 cups and add 1/4 cup unsweetened cocoa powder and 1/2 cup miniature semisweet chocolate chips to the batter before baking.

PALEO POWER PUCKS

1 large egg white

1 tablespoon honey, agave nectar, or maple syrup

1/4 teaspoon ground cinnamon

1/4 teaspoon fine sea salt

1 cup chopped nuts (e.g., walnuts, pecans, almonds)

1/2 cup seeds (e.g., sunflower, pumpkin, hemp hearts)

1/3 cup chopped dried fruit (e.g., dates, prunes, apricots)

The Paleo Diet, also known as the Stone Age Diet or Caveman Diet, is gaining momentum in the fitness world as a healthy way to eat well and lose weight. The crux of the meal plan is to follow the dietary habits of our Paleolithic, cave-dwelling ancestors: specifically, wild game, meat, eggs, and seafood, and vegetables, fruit, seeds, and nuts. Absent from the diet are foods that developed during the agricultural and industrial eras such as grains, dairy, legumes, refined sugars, and any other processed foods. While I am no expert on caveman snacking habits, I feel certain these crispy, crunchy, mildly sweet power pucks would receive an enthusiastic, prehensile thumb up. **MAKES 10 PUCKS**

1. Line 10 cups of a 12-cup muffin pan with paper or foil liners.

2. Preheat oven to 325°F.

3. Whisk the egg white, honey, cinnamon, and salt in a medium bowl until blended. Add the nuts, seeds, and dried fruit, stirring until completely combined.

4. Divide the mixture evenly in the prepared muffin cups.

5. Bake in the preheated oven for 16 to 20 minutes or until golden brown. Transfer to a wire rack and cool completely.

Nutrients per puck: Calories 113, Fat 8.6 g, (Saturated 0.5 g), Cholesterol 0 mg, Sodium 65 mg, Carbs 7.3 g (Fiber 1.2 g, Sugars 4.8 g), Protein 4.0 g

BAR TIPS

—If you are not following a strictly Paleo diet, feel free to add 1/2 teaspoon vanilla extract or 1/4 teaspoon almond extract to the egg white mixture.

—If you are following a strictly Paleo diet, be sure to use unsweetened or fruit juice-sweetened dried fruit.

—Vary the types of ground spices to your heart's content. Ground ginger, cardamom, or pumpkin pie spice are delicious alternatives to cinnamon.

—Lining the muffin tin cups with paper or foil liners promotes even browning and keeps the edges of the pucks from over-browning or burning.

—Feel free to alter the proportions of nuts and seeds; just keep the total amount to 1 1/2 cups. You can also use all seeds or all nuts.

—To make the pucks sugar-free, omit the honey. Use two egg whites and add 1/2 teaspoon liquid stevia.

BAR KEEPING

Tightly wrap the pucks individually in plastic wrap.

ROOM TEMP: 5 days
REFRIGERATOR: 2 weeks
FREEZER: 3 months in airtight container; thaw 30 minutes

BAR VARIATIONS

TROPICAL PALEO PUCKS

Add 2 teaspoons finely grated lime zest to the egg white mixture and replace the cinnamon with an equal amount of ground ginger. Replace the dried fruit with 1/2 cup unsweetened flake or shredded coconut.

CHOCOLATE PALEO PUCKS

Omit the cinnamon and add 2 teaspoons natural, unsweetened cocoa powder to the egg white mixture. Replace the dried fruit with 1/4 cup finely chopped dates and 3 tablespoons cacao nibs.

SALTY-SPICY-SWEET NUT PUCKS

Omit the seeds and dried fruit and use 1 3/4 cups assorted chopped nuts. Replace the cinnamon with an equal amount of pumpkin pie spice or ground allspice.

ROSEMARY GOLDEN RAISIN PUCKS

Omit the cinnamon and add 2 teaspoons finely chopped fresh rosemary leaves and 2 teaspoons finely grated lemon zest. Use golden raisins for the dried fruit.

CHERRY PIE PALEO PUCKS

Omit the seeds and use 3/4 cup chopped pecans or walnuts and 3/4 cup chopped almonds for the nuts. Use dried cherries for the dried fruit. If desired, add 1/2 teaspoon vanilla extract to the egg white mixture.

PROTEIN
BARS

Looking to control appetite, build muscle, and repair muscle following exercise? Then you have turned to the right chapter. What sets these protein bars apart from the majority of ready-made bars is their high-quality protein: all-natural whey or vegan protein powders and whole foods that are naturally high in protein such as quinoa, beans, nuts, and seeds. High-quality ingredients have a consequence that further differentiates these bars from store-bought: deliciousness. From brownies to banana blondies to chocolate chip cookies, the recipes in this chapter raise the bar for great taste, renewed energy, and muscle power.

BLACK BEAN
HIGH PROTEIN BROWNIES

1 15-ounce can unseasoned black beans, very well-rinsed and drained

1/3 cup agave nectar or pure maple syrup

3 large eggs

1/3 cup low-fat milk

3 tablespoons virgin coconut oil, warmed until melted, or vegetable oil

2 teaspoons instant espresso powder

1 teaspoon vanilla extract

3/4 cup lightly packed all-natural, sweetened chocolate or vanilla whey protein powder

1/4 cup unsweetened, natural cocoa powder

3/4 teaspoon baking powder

1/4 teaspoon fine sea salt

1/3 cup miniature semisweet or bittersweet chocolate chips

If totally fudgy, chocolate goodness is what you crave in a protein bar, then this recipe is for you. If you have not heard of black bean brownies before now, I understand the wariness—beans+chocolate=brownie sounds like new math gone terribly wrong. But then you take a bite and realize that everything about these bars is 100% right. Some black bean brownie recipes try to take out all of the fat and the sweetener, which, while noble, leads to a pan of cocoa-flavored bean squares. By contrast, my version keeps a reasonable amount of fats and sweeteners, balancing it out with maximal protein (eggs+protein powder+beans), which leads to pan full of deliciousness. The choice is yours, my friend. **MAKES 12 BARS**

1. Line a 9-inch square baking pan with foil or parchment paper and spray with nonstick cooking spray.

2. Preheat oven to 350°F.

3. Place the beans, agave nectar, eggs, milk, oil, espresso powder, and vanilla in a food processor. Process, using on/off pulses, until the mixture is blended and completely smooth, stopping to scrape the sides and bottom of the bowl several times with a rubber spatula.

4. Add the protein powder, cocoa powder, baking powder, and salt to the bowl; process using on/off pulses until all of the protein powder is incorporated, stopping to scrape the sides and bottom of the bowl once or twice with a rubber spatula.

5. Spread the batter evenly in the prepared pan; sprinkle with the chocolate chips.

6. Bake in the preheated oven for 25 to 30 minutes or until the top appears somewhat dry and the edges begin to pull away from the sides of the pan. Transfer to a wire rack and cool completely.

7. Using the liner, lift the mixture from the pan and transfer to a cutting board. Cut into 12 bars. Store in the refrigerator or freezer.

Nutrients per bar: Calories 166, Fat 7 g, (Saturated 4.7 g), Cholesterol 60 mg, Sodium 87 mg, Carbs 17.9 g (Fiber 2.4 g, Sugars 11.4 g), Protein 9.5 g

BAR TIPS

—These brownies will look different from conventional brownies in two ways when they are done: first, the top will look much drier, and second, the center will feel gooier when lightly touched. Once cool, though, they are fudgy, not dry; the center will set up once the bars are completely cooled (and even more so when refrigerated).

—Pinto beans or soft white beans (e.g., cannellini or Great Northern beans) can be used with equal success in place of the black beans.

—For a lower sugar brownie, omit the agave nectar and add 1 1/2 teaspoons liquid stevia. Increase the total amount of milk to 2/3 cup.

—1 tablespoon coffee powder (regular or decaffeinated) may be used in place of the espresso powder.

BAR KEEPING

Tightly wrap the bars individually in plastic wrap.

REFRIGERATOR: 1 week
FREEZER: 3 months in airtight container; thaw 1 hour

BAR VARIATIONS

MOCHA ALMOND PROTEIN BROWNIES
Increase the espresso powder to 1 tablespoon and replace the vanilla extract with an equal amount of almond extract.

CHOCOLATE-CHERRY PROTEIN BROWNIES
Replace the vanilla extract with an equal amount of almond extract and add 1/2 cup chopped dried cherries to the batter.

VEGAN BLACK BEAN BROWNIES
Use vegan protein powder in place of the whey powder and plain nondairy milk in place of the milk. Additionally, replace the eggs with flaxseed or chia "eggs": combine 3 tablespoons flaxseed meal or chia seeds with 1/2 cup plus 1 tablespoon warm water, then let stand 5 minutes to thicken.

DARK CHOCOLATE PEANUT BUTTER PROTEIN BARS

RECIPE PAGE 110

BLACK BEAN HIGH PROTEIN BROWNIES

RECIPE PAGE 106

CHOCOLATE CHIP PROTEIN COOKIES

RECIPE PAGE 112

BANANA BLONDIE
PROTEIN PUCKS

RECIPE
PAGE
114

DARK CHOCOLATE PEANUT BUTTER PROTEIN BARS

1/2 cup roasted, lightly salted peanuts

1/2 cup natural, unsweetened peanut butter

1/2 cup plain nondairy milk or low-fat dairy milk

1/4 cup virgin coconut oil, warmed until melted

1 teaspoon vanilla extract

1 2/3 cup lightly packed all-natural, sweetened chocolate vegan protein powder

1/4 cup unsweetened, natural cocoa powder

PEANUT BUTTER ICING

1/4 cup natural, unsweetened peanut butter

2 tablespoons plain nondairy milk or low-fat dairy milk

1 tablespoon virgin coconut oil

1/4 teaspoon liquid stevia

1/4 teaspoon vanilla extract

1/8 teaspoon fine sea salt

A peanut butter and chocolate combination is probably what springs to mind when you think of protein bars. And if you glance at the shelves of protein bars at the supermarket, health food, and athletic stores, you might think it is the only flavor combination (chocolate-peanut butter, peanut butter-chocolate, double peanut butter chocolate fudge, fudgy chocolate peanut butter blast...you get the idea). Infractions abound—notably those sporting choco- (make that chalk-oh) flavor coatings and gum-enhanced fillings—but a fantastic peanut butter-chocolate protein bar is worth pursuing. Lucky you, the pursuit is over. Whenever you want a trustworthy, taste-worthy peanut butter and chocolate bar, this is it. **MAKES 12 BARS**

1. Line an 8-inch square baking pan with foil or parchment paper and spray with nonstick cooking spray.

2. Place the peanuts in a food processor and process into a fine powder (not a paste). Add the peanut butter, milk, oil, and vanilla. Process, using on/off pulses, until the mixture is blended, stopping to scrape the sides and bottom of the bowl several times with a rubber spatula.

3. Add the protein powder and cocoa powder to bowl; process using on/off pulses until all of the protein powder is incorporated, stopping to scrape the sides and bottom of the bowl once or twice with a rubber spatula.

4. Transfer the mixture to the prepared pan. Place a large piece of parchment paper, wax paper, or plastic wrap (coated with nonstick cooking spray) atop the bar mixture and use it to spread and flatten the mixture evenly in the pan.

5. To prepare the icing: In a small saucepan, combine the peanut butter, milk, and coconut oil. Heat over medium-low, stirring, for 1 to 2 minutes until mixture is melted and smooth. Remove from heat and stir in the stevia, vanilla, and

Nutrients per bar: Calories 271, Fat 21.2 g, (Saturated 10.2 g), Cholesterol 30 mg, Sodium 101 mg, Carbs 7.2 g (Fiber 2.8 g, Sugars 2.5 g), Protein 16 g

salt; immediately pour and spread over the bar mixture. Cover and refrigerate overnight until very firm.

6. Using the liner, lift the mixture from the pan and transfer to a cutting board. Uncover and cut into 12 bars. Store in the refrigerator or freezer.

BAR TIPS

—Coconut oil adds a subtle coconut flavor to these bars, but it also helps to hold them together. Vegetable oil will not work in its place.

—Protein powders vary in terms of their dryness. Hence, if the mixture seems too wet, add a bit more protein powder, or some ground oats or flaxseed meal, until the mixture comes together as a dough. It the mixture seems too dry, add some milk (nondairy or dairy) or water, one tablespoon at a time, until the mixture comes together as a dough.

—Whey protein will not work as a measure for measure replacement in this recipe. However, you can use a combination of 1 cup whey protein powder and 3/4 cup rolled oats, processed to a fine powder, in place of the vegan protein powder.

—An equal amount of any other natural nut or seed butter may be used in place of the peanut butter and an equal amount of any other nuts or seeds may be used in place of the peanuts.

—1 tablespoon of any liquid sweetener (e.g., maple syrup, honey, or agave nectar) may be used in place of the stevia in the peanut butter icing. Decrease the total amount of milk to 1 1/2 tablespoons.

BAR KEEPING

Tightly wrap the bars individually in plastic wrap.

REFRIGERATOR: 1 week
FREEZER: 3 months in airtight container; thaw 1 hour

CHOCOLATE CHIP
PROTEIN COOKIES

1 15-ounce can unseasoned white beans (e.g., cannellini or Great Northern), very well-rinsed and drained

1/2 cup natural, unsweetened nut or seed butter (e.g., peanut, cashew, sunflower, or tahini)

1/4 cup plain nondairy milk or low-fat dairy milk

1/4 cup flaxseed meal

2 teaspoons vanilla extract

1 1/4 teaspoons liquid stevia

1 teaspoon ground cinnamon

1 teaspoon baking powder

1/3 cup miniature semisweet or bittersweet chocolate chips

Nothing beats a chocolate chip cookie to satisfy a sweet tooth, make you feel like a kid again, and generally make the world a brighter, happier place. These amazing cookies do all of that and then some: high in protein and fiber, sugar-free (save for a small smattering of miniature chocolate chips), easy on the wallet, and a quick-as-a-jiffy assembly to boot. If the thought of chocolate chip cookies made from canned beans still sounds wrong to you, I promise after one or two cookies, you'll concur that it's completely right. MAKES 24 COOKIES

1. Line a large cookie sheet with parchment paper.

2. Preheat oven to 375°F.

3. Place the beans, nut or seed butter, milk, flaxseed meal, vanilla, stevia, cinnamon, and baking powder in a food processor. Process, using on/off pulses, until the mixture is blended and completely smooth, stopping to scrape the sides and bottom of the bowl several times with a rubber spatula.

4. Transfer the dough to a medium bowl and stir in the chocolate chips.

5. Drop the dough by tablespoonfuls onto the prepared cookie sheet, spacing them 2 inches apart. Flatten each cookie with the tines of a fork that has been dipped in water.

6. Bake in the preheated oven for 13 to 17 minutes or until golden brown at the edges and on top. Let cool on the sheet on a wire rack for 5 minutes, then place cookies directly onto the rack to cool completely. Store in the refrigerator or freezer.

Nutrients per cookie: Calories 68, Fat 3.9 g, (Saturated 1 g), Cholesterol 0 mg, Sodium 32 mg, Carbs 5.1 g (Fiber 1.7 g, Sugars 1.5 g), Protein 3 g

BAR TIPS

—The cookies will still seem somewhat soft when they are ready to be removed from the oven (it is because they are flourless cookies), so use color—in this case, a golden brown color at the edges and on top—to determine doneness. The cookies will continue to firm up as they cool.

—In place of the stevia, 3 1/2 tablespoons of natural cane sugar or packed organic light brown sugar may be used; other liquid sweeteners will make the dough gooey and the cookies will not set up.

BAR KEEPING

Tightly wrap the cookies individually in plastic wrap.

REFRIGERATOR: 5 days
FREEZER: 3 months in airtight container; thaw 1 hour

BAR VARIATIONS

CHOCOLATE FUDGE PROTEIN COOKIES
Increase the milk to 1/3 cup and replace the flaxseed meal with 3 tablespoons unsweetened, natural cocoa powder (not Dutch process).

CHOCOLATE-MINT FUDGE PROTEIN COOKIES
Increase the milk to 1/3 cup and replace the flaxseed meal with 3 tablespoons unsweetened, natural cocoa powder (not Dutch process). Replace the vanilla extract with an equal amount of peppermint extract.

CHAI SPICE PROTEIN COOKIES
Use 3/4 teaspoon ground ginger, 1/2 teaspoon ground cinnamon, and 1/4 teaspoon ground cardamom in place of the 1 teaspoon cinnamon. Use 1/3 cup finely chopped, pitted, soft dates in place of the chocolate chips.

ALMOND JOYFUL PROTEIN COOKIES
Use an equal amount of almond extract in place of the vanilla extract and omit the cinnamon. Replace the flaxseed meal with 1/3 cup unsweetened flake or shredded coconut (toasted or untoasted), finely chopped.

BANANA BLONDIE
PROTEIN PUCKS

1 cup almonds, raw or toasted (see tips)

1 1/4 cups mashed, very ripe bananas

3 large eggs

2 large egg whites

1 cup lightly packed all-natural, sweetened vanilla whey protein powder

1 teaspoon baking powder

1/4 teaspoon fine sea salt

As a general rule, I like my banana baked goods unimpeded: no lumps, bumps, or chunks. Case in point, these protein pucks. Luscious and rich, they are worthy of their blondie eponym. But just because I like these pucks sans-accessories doesn't mean you can't gussy them up any and every which way, so add up to 1/2 cup chocolate chips, nuts, or dried fruit if lumpy-bumpy-chunky is your style. **MAKES 12 PUCKS**

1. Spray a 12-cup muffin pan with nonstick cooking spray.

2. Preheat oven to 325°F.

3. Place the almonds in a food processor and process until finely chopped (but not a paste). Add the bananas, eggs, egg whites, protein powder, baking powder, and salt. Process, using on/off pulses, until blended and smooth.

4. Divide the batter evenly in the prepared muffin cups.

5. Bake in the preheated oven for 20 to 25 minutes or until the edges are golden and the center is just set when touched. Transfer to a wire rack and cool completely. Remove from pan and store in the refrigerator or freezer.

Nutrients per puck: Calories 128, Fat 5.9 g, (Saturated 1.1 g), Cholesterol 64 mg, Sodium 118 mg, Carbs 8.8 g (Fiber 1.6 g, Sugars 4.5 g), Protein 11.2 g

BAR TIPS

—You can use 1 cup plus 1 tablespoon ready-made almond flour or almond meal in place of grinding the almonds. If desired, you can lightly toast the almond flour in a large, dry, nonstick skillet set over medium heat: cook and stir the flour until it turns golden and fragrant, about 2 to 3 minutes.

—You can use an equal amount of other nuts or seeds in place of the almonds.

—Be sure to use extremely ripe bananas (the peels should be almost entirely brown) for the best result In this recipe. It will take about three to four medium-large, extra-ripe bananas to yield the 1 1/4 cups mashed bananas called for in the recipe.

—3/4 cup all-natural, sweetened vanilla vegan protein powder may be used in place of the whey protein powder.

BAR KEEPING

Tightly wrap the pucks individually in plastic wrap.

REFRIGERATOR: 5 days
FREEZER: 1 month in airtight container; thaw 1 hour

BAR VARIATIONS

BANANA SPLIT PROTEIN PUCKS
Add 3 tablespoons miniature semisweet chocolate chips, 3 tablespoons chopped dried cherries, and 1 tablespoon chopped peanuts to the batter.

DOUBLE CHOCOLATE BANANA PUCKS
Use an equal amount of chocolate protein powder in place of the vanilla and add 1/2 teaspoon almond extract to the batter.

PB & J PROTEIN FIBER BARS

1 cup packed pitted, soft dates

1 cup warm water

1/3 cup low-fat milk or plain nondairy milk

1/4 cup natural, unsweetened peanut butter

1 cup lightly packed all-natural, sweetened vanilla whey protein powder

1/2 cup barley and wheat nugget cereal (e.g., Grape-Nuts®)

1/2 cup dried cherries, dried cranberries, or dried strawberries, finely chopped

1/4 cup flaxseed meal

I've been there. Trying to transport a peanut butter and jelly sandwich on a long trek by foot, train, plane, or automobile. It looks sturdy as can be on the mega-grain bread you purchased specifically for the task. You wrap it securely, then into the backpack, briefcase, or purse it goes, gently positioned out of harm's way. You feel smug. And then you reach into your bag, and oh my god, what happened? It's a veritable PB & J massacre. But hold everything, it doesn't have to be that way! You can have your homemade, multigrain PB & J in a tidy, portable package. I don't think I need to tell you that they are darn delicious, too. Do I? OK. PB & J Protein Fiber Bars are darn delicious! **MAKES 12 BARS**

1. Line an 8-inch square baking pan with foil or parchment paper and spray with nonstick cooking spray.

2. Combine the dates and warm water in a small bowl. Let stand for 5 to 10 minutes until dates are soft (time will vary according to the dryness of the dates). Drain and pat dry with paper towels.

3. Place the drained dates, milk, and peanut butter in a food processor and process until blended and smooth.

4. Add the protein powder to the bowl; process using on/off pulses until all of the protein powder is incorporated, stopping to scrape the sides and bottom of the bowl once or twice with a rubber spatula. Transfer the mixture to a large bowl.

5. Fold the cereal, cherries, and flaxseed meal into the date mixture, mixing with a spatula until well blended.

6. Transfer the mixture to the prepared pan. Place a large piece of parchment paper, wax paper, or plastic wrap (coated with nonstick cooking spray) atop the bar mixture and use it to spread and flatten the mixture evenly in the pan; leave the paper or plastic wrap to cover. Refrigerate at least 4 hours or overnight.

7. Using the liner, lift the mixture from the pan and transfer to a cutting board. Uncover and cut into 12 bars. Store in the refrigerator or freezer.

Nutrients per bar: Calories 170, Fat 4.5 g, (Saturated 1 g), Cholesterol 17 mg, Sodium 72 mg, Carbs 22 g (Fiber 3.7 g, Sugars 15.2 g), Protein 10.7 g

BAR TIPS

—Peanut butter is the classic choice for these bars, but feel free to use any natural, unsweetened nut or seed butter (e.g., almond, cashew, sunflower, or tahini) in its place.

—3/4 cup all-natural, sweetened vanilla vegan protein powder may be used in place of the whey protein powder.

BAR KEEPING

Tightly wrap the bars individually in plastic wrap.

ROOM TEMP: 3 days
REFRIGERATOR: 5 days
FREEZER: 3 months in airtight container; thaw 1 hour

BAR VARIATIONS

PEANUT BUTTER-CHOCOLATE CHIP PROTEIN BARS

Replace the dried cherries with 1/3 cup miniature semisweet chocolate chips or cacao nibs.

ALMOND-APRICOT PROTEIN BARS

Use an equal amount of natural, unsweetened almond butter in place of the peanut butter and an equal amount of dried apricots in place of the cherries. Add 1 teaspoon almond extract along with the peanut butter.

GLUTEN-FREE PB & J BARS

You can easily make these bars gluten-free by swapping the nugget cereal for an equal amount of gluten-free brown rice cereal, gluten-free rolled oats, or gluten-free granola (chopped or coarsely crushed before measuring).

CHOCOLATE-COVERED RAISIN PROTEIN BARS

Use an equal amount of all-natural, sweetened chocolate whey or vegan protein powder in place of the vanilla protein powder. Use 3 tablespoons unsweetened, natural cocoa powder (not Dutch process) in place of the flaxseed meal and an equal amount of raisins in place of the dried cherries.

5-MINUTE PROTEIN TRUFFLES

1/2 cup natural, unsweetened nut or seed butter (e.g., peanut, cashew, sunflower, or tahini)

3 tablespoons honey, agave nectar, or pure maple syrup

1/8 teaspoon fine sea salt

2/3 cup lightly packed all-natural, sweetened vanilla whey protein powder

SUGGESTED COATINGS (OPTIONAL):

— Miniature semisweet chocolate chips or cacao nibs

— Unsweetened, natural cocoa powder

— Unsweetened flake or shredded coconut, plain or toasted

— Finely chopped toasted or raw nuts (e.g., almonds, walnuts, pistachios, hazelnuts)

— Toasted or raw seeds, finely chopped if needed (e.g., sesame, chia, pepitas, hemp hearts, sunflower)

— Finely chopped dried fruit (e.g., cherries, raisins, apricots, blueberries)

—Matcha powder

—Quick-cooking rolled oats

These protein "truffles" are so ridiculously easy that I feel somewhat silly adding them to this collection. Then again, my super-simple, silly recipes are often my most popular. They are certainly favorites in my repertoire, in large part because of their fast factor, but also because of their portability and candy-like appeal. Plus, they are endlessly customizable by varying the spices, extracts, and other add-ins, or by giving them a chic coating of chia seeds, cocoa powder, or chopped nuts. Who says pretty and power can't go together? MAKES ABOUT 12 1-INCH BALLS

1. Mix the nut or seed butter, honey, and salt in a medium bowl until blended. Add the protein powder, stirring until completely combined (mixture will be firm).

2. Protein powders vary in terms of their dryness. Hence if the mixture seems too wet, add a bit more protein powder, or some ground oats or flaxseed meal, until the mixture comes together as a dough. If the mixture seems too dry, add some milk (nondairy or dairy) or water, one tablespoon at a time, until the mixture comes together as a dough.

3. Scoop about 1 1/2 tablespoons of the mixture into your hands and shape into 1-inch balls.

4. If desired, place one or more of the suggested coatings in small shallow dishes. Roll each ball in the coating, gently pressing to adhere. Place the balls in an airtight container and store in the refrigerator.

BAR TIPS

—If you prefer, mix up to 3 tablespoons of any of the suggested coatings directly into the dough instead of using as a coating.

—A box of these beauties makes a great hostess gift or present in general, especially to the fitness and health foodie friends in your life.

—1/2 cup all-natural, sweetened vanilla or chocolate vegan protein powder may be used in place of the whey protein powder.

BAR KEEPING

Store in an airtight container.

REFRIGERATOR: 1 week
FREEZER: 3 months in airtight container; thaw 15 minutes

Nutrients per truffle: Calories 109, Fat 5.8 g, (Saturated 1.2 g), Cholesterol 11 mg, Sodium 52 mg, Carbs 7.2 g (Fiber 0.7 g, Sugars 5.6 g), Protein 7.9 g

BAR VARIATIONS

CHOCOLATE PEANUT BUTTER PROTEIN BALLS

Use peanut butter for the nut butter and chocolate protein powder in place of the vanilla protein powder. Add 1 1/2 tablespoons unsweetened, natural cocoa powder (not Dutch process) and 1 1/2 tablespoons water along with the honey.

MOCHA JAVA BALLS

Use chocolate protein powder in place of the vanilla protein powder. Add 2 teaspoons instant espresso powder, dissolved in 2 teaspoons warm water, along with the honey.

GINGERBREAD PROTEIN BALLS

Use 3 tablespoons dark (cooking) molasses for the sweetener and add 1/2 teaspoon ground cinnamon, 1/4 teaspoon ground ginger, and 1/8 teaspoon ground cloves along with the protein powder.

SNICKERDOODLE PROTEIN BALLS

Add 3/4 teaspoon ground cinnamon and 1/8 teaspoon ground nutmeg along with the protein powder. Add 3 tablespoons chopped raisins to the dough before rolling into balls. Roll the balls in finely chopped toasted pecans or walnuts.

REAL FRUIT PROTEIN BARS

1 cup packed dried fruit (e.g., apricots, cranberries, cherries, figs)

1 cup warm water

1 1/2 cups old-fashioned or quick-cooking rolled oats

1 cup lightly packed all-natural, sweetened vanilla whey protein powder

3 tablespoons low-fat milk

2 teaspoons finely grated lemon zest or orange zest (optional)

I don't know about you, but nothing says delicious fruit flavor to me more than ethyl valerate, isobutyl butyrate, 4-methylacetophenone, and heliotropin (this last one is also a common perfume ingredient—you can smell pretty inside and out!). All kidding aside, those are just a few of the icky ingredients used to make the artificial "fruit" flavoring in several high-protein bars on the market. But wait, here's a crazy notion: why not use real fruit? I tried it, and guess what? It works. With all of the wonderful, all-natural dried fruits available these days, the possibilities for variation are extensive. Hurray for fruit! MAKES 6 BARS

1. Line a 9 by 5-inch loaf pan with plastic wrap and spray with nonstick cooking spray.

2. Combine the fruit and warm water in a small bowl. Let stand for 5 to 10 minutes until fruit is soft (time will vary according to the dryness of the fruit). Drain and pat dry with paper towels.

3. Meanwhile, place the oats in a food processor and process into a fine powder. Add the drained fruit, protein powder, milk, and lemon zest, if using. Process, using on/off pulses, until the fruit is finely chopped and blended and the mixture begins to stick together and clump on the sides of the bowl.

4. Transfer the mixture to the prepared pan. Place a piece of parchment paper, wax paper, or plastic wrap (coated with nonstick cooking spray) atop the bar mixture and use it to spread and flatten the mixture evenly in the pan; leave the paper or plastic wrap to cover. Refrigerate for 30 minutes.

5. Using the liner, lift the mixture from the pan and transfer to a cutting board. Uncover and cut into 6 bars.

Nutrients per bar: Calories 252, Fat 2.6 g, (Saturated 0.9 g), Cholesterol 33 mg, Sodium 93 mg, Carbs 40.8 g (Fiber 41 g, Sugars 23.2 g), Protein 16.7 g

BAR TIPS

—Try adding up to 1/2 teaspoon of your favorite ground spice to the mixture, such as cinnamon, ginger, or cardamom.

—Dried apples do not work well in this recipe (due to their texture), but if you happen upon dried pears, try them. They work like a dream and are unbelievably good.

BAR KEEPING

Tightly wrap the bars individually in plastic wrap.

ROOM TEMP: 2 days
REFRIGERATOR: 1 week
FREEZER: 3 months in airtight container; thaw I hour

BAR VARIATIONS

CHOCOLATE-APRICOT PROTEIN BARS
Use an equal amount of chocolate vegan protein powder in place of the vanilla protein powder and use dried apricots for the fruit. Add 1/2 teaspoon almond extract along with the fruit and use orange zest.

BLUEBERRY PIE PROTEIN BARS
Use dried blueberries for the fruit. Add 1/2 teaspoon almond extract along with the fruit and use lemon zest.

LEMON POPPY SEED PROTEIN BARS
Use golden raisins for the fruit. Add 2 tablespoons poppy seeds along with the fruit and use lemon zest.

VEGAN FRUIT PROTEIN BARS
Use vegan protein powder instead of the whey protein powder and decrease the oats to 1 cup. Use nondairy milk in place of the dairy milk.

SALTY-SWEET TRAIL BARS

1 1/2 cups quick-cooking rolled oats or quinoa flakes

3/4 cup crisp puffed brown rice cereal

2/3 cup lightly packed all-natural, sweetened vanilla whey or vegan protein powder

1/4 cup roasted, lightly salted pepitas (green pumpkin seeds)

1/4 cup roasted, lightly salted sunflower seeds

1/4 cup chia seeds

1/4 cup unsweetened flake or shredded coconut, finely chopped

1/2 cup agave nectar, honey, or pure maple syrup

1/2 cup natural, unsweetened nut or seed butter (e.g., peanut, cashew, or sunflower)

3 tablespoons plain nondairy milk or low-fat milk

1 teaspoon vanilla extract

Chocolate or White Chocolate Bar Coating (optional; see page 31)

I love a good hike on a foggy Bay Area morning or a sunny Texas afternoon (so long as the latter is not in mid-July), but I'm a bit of a baby when it comes to hauling around an über-heavy backpack. I prefer packing light with some water, snacks, and a few band-aids, all that I need before hitting the trail. Rather than fuss over whether I'll be craving a sweet or a salty snack, I cover both bases with these easy, protein-pumped bars. They have the added virtue of a super-quick prep-time (that's right—you can procrastinate and make them the day of the hike with time to spare). Follow my lead with the assortment of seeds or create your own backpacking bar-blend. **MAKES 12 BARS**

1. Line a 9-inch square baking pan with foil or parchment paper and spray with nonstick cooking spray.

2. Stir together the oats, cereal, protein powder, pepitas, sunflower seeds, chia seeds, and coconut in a large bowl.

3. In a small saucepan, combine the agave nectar, nut or seed butter, and milk. Heat over medium-low, stirring, for 2 to 4 minutes, until mixture is melted and bubbly. Remove from heat and stir in the vanilla.

4. Immediately pour the agave mixture over the oats mixture, mixing with a spatula until coated.

5. Transfer the mixture to the prepared pan. Place a large piece of parchment paper, wax paper, or plastic wrap (coated with nonstick cooking spray) atop the bar mixture and use it to spread, flatten, and very firmly compact the mixture evenly in the pan. Cool completely. If desired, spread or drizzle with the bar coating. Refrigerate at least two hours until very firm.

6. Using the liner, lift the mixture from the pan and transfer to a cutting board. Cut into 12 bars.

Nutrients per bar: Calories 219, Fat 9.7 g, (Saturated 2.5 g), Cholesterol 11 mg, Sodium 62 mg, Carbs 23.2 g (Fiber 3.8 g, Sugars 12.6 g), Protein 10.8 g

BAR TIPS

—I like to use already-roasted, lightly salted seeds in this recipe to keep the assembly time down to about 5 minutes flat, but raw seeds or nuts are delicious here, too. Alternatively, toast the raw seeds or nuts by spreading them on a large rimmed baking sheet and baking in a preheated 350°F oven for 6 to 8 minutes, shaking halfway through, until golden and fragrant. Add 1/4 teaspoon fine sea salt.

—An equal amount of any variety of puffed or crisp whole-grain cereal—millet, amaranth, multigrain, quinoa—can be used in place of the crisp brown rice cereal.

BAR KEEPING

Tightly wrap the bars individually in plastic wrap.

ROOM TEMP: 3 days
REFRIGERATOR: 1 week
FREEZER: 3 months in airtight container; thaw 1 hour

BAR VARIATIONS

SPICY CHOCOLATE TRAIL-BLAZING BARS

Use an equal amount of chocolate protein powder in place of the vanilla protein powder. Omit the sunflower seeds and chia seeds and add 1/2 cup cacao nibs or miniature semisweet chocolate chips along with the oats. Add 1 teaspoon ground cinnamon and 1/4 teaspoon cayenne pepper along with the vanilla.

CRANBERRY-PEPITA TRAIL BARS

Omit the sunflower seeds, chia seeds, and coconut. Increase the total amount of pepitas to 1/2 cup and add 1/2 cup dried cranberries, chopped. Replace the vanilla with an equal amount of almond extract.

SWEET POTATO PROTEIN BARS

2 large sweet potatoes (about 1 1/3 pounds)

2 cups old-fashioned or quick-cooking rolled oats

1 cup lightly packed all-natural, sweetened vanilla whey protein powder

1/4 cup low-fat milk or plain nondairy milk

1/4 cup pure maple syrup, agave nectar, or honey

2 teaspoons vanilla extract

1 1/2 teaspoons ground cinnamon

1/4 teaspoon fine sea salt

I happen to think that almost anything made with sweet potatoes is worth eating, but these quick and easy protein bars, enhanced with maple syrup and cinnamon, are extra-easy to adore. In addition to tasting great, sweet potatoes are highly nutritious: they are an excellent source of vitamin A (in the form of beta-carotene), a very good source of vitamin C and manganese, and a good source of copper, dietary fiber, vitamin B6, potassium, and iron. MAKES 8 BARS

1. Line an 8-inch square baking pan with foil or parchment paper and spray with nonstick cooking spray.

2. Prick the sweet potatoes all over with a fork. Place on a large plate and microwave on High, turning over every 5 minutes, for 15 to 20 minutes or until very soft. Immediately slice in half to let steam escape. When cool enough to handle, scoop the flesh into a bowl and mash with a fork until you have a very smooth purée. Cool completely, and then measure out 1 1/4 cups. Any remaining purée can be frozen in an airtight container for future use.

3. Place the oats in a food processor and process into a fine powder.

4. Add the sweet potato purée, protein powder, milk, maple syrup, vanilla, cinnamon, and salt to the processor bowl. Process, using on/off pulses, until the mixture is blended, stopping to scrape the sides and bottom of the bowl once or twice with a rubber spatula.

5. Transfer the mixture to the prepared pan. Place a large piece of parchment paper, wax paper, or plastic wrap (coated with nonstick cooking spray) atop the bar mixture and use it to spread and flatten the mixture evenly in the pan. Cover and refrigerate overnight until very firm.

6 . Using the liner, lift the mixture from the pan and transfer to a cutting board. Uncover and cut into 8 bars. Store in the refrigerator or freezer.

Nutrients per bar: Calories 195, Fat 2.4 g, (Saturated 0.7 g), Cholesterol 25 mg, Sodium 98 mg, Carbs 29.8 g (Fiber 3.2 g, Sugars 10.8 g), Protein 14 g

BAR TIP

—You have two simple alternatives to making your own sweet potato purée. First, head to the baby food section of the supermarket and get 3 four-ounce jars of organic sweet potato baby food. (Fear not: the extent of the ingredients is organic sweet potatoes and water.) Two and one-half jars will yield the required 1 1/4 cups of purée. Second, health food stores, as well as online sources, offer canned organic sweet potato purée.

BAR KEEPING

Tightly wrap the bars individually in plastic wrap.

REFRIGERATOR: 5 days
FREEZER: 3 months in airtight container; thaw 1 hour

BAR VARIATIONS

SUGAR-FREE SWEET POTATO BARS
Omit the maple syrup and increase the milk to 1/2 cup. Add 1 1/4 teaspoons liquid stevia along with the milk.

PUMPKIN PROTEIN BARS
Replace sweet potatoes with an equal amount of pumpkin purée (not pie filling).

SWEET POTATO PECAN POWER BARS
Use 1/4 cup dark (cooking) molasses for the sweetener. Add 1/2 cup toasted pecans along with the sweet potato purée.

VEGAN SWEET POTATO BARS
Use 3/4 cup all-natural, sweetened vanilla vegan protein powder in place of the whey protein powder. Use nondairy milk and either maple syrup or agave nectar.

QUINOA PROTEIN BARS

1/3 cup quinoa, rinsed

1/2 cup water

1 cup old-fashioned or quick-cooking rolled oats

1/2 cup flaxseed meal

1/2 cup lightly packed all-natural, sweetened vanilla vegan protein powder

1/4 teaspoon fine sea salt

1/3 cup pure maple syrup, agave nectar, or honey

3 tablespoons virgin coconut oil, warmed until melted

3 tablespoons plain nondairy milk or low-fat dairy milk

By now, almost everyone has encountered a quinoa salad at a potluck party (it's virtually inevitable if you are married to an English professor—as my husband likes to quip, quinoa tabbouleh is the new hummus in academic circles). But if you think salad is the extent of cooked quinoa, then step right up to the bar. A quinoa protein bar, that is. It turns out that quinoa is an ideal power bar ingredient: loaded with vitamins, minerals, and protein (complete protein, no less; the only plant with such a profile), high in fiber, naturally nutty flavor, and minimal prep time. People who are on the fence about quinoa will have their faith restored, while those who already love it will be blissed out. Enjoy. **MAKES 9 BARS**

1. Line an 8-inch square baking pan with foil or parchment paper and spray with nonstick cooking spray.

2. Combine the quinoa and water in a small saucepan. Bring to a boil over medium-high heat. Reduce heat to low, cover, and simmer for 9 to 13 minutes or until liquid is just barely absorbed. Remove from heat. Cover and let stand for 5 to 6 minutes. Remove lid and fluff with a fork. Transfer to a large bowl and cool completely.

3. Add the oats, flaxseed meal, protein powder, and salt to the quinoa, stirring until combined.

4. Whisk the maple syrup, oil, and milk in a small bowl until blended.

5. Add the maple mixture to the oats mixture, stirring with a spatula until well blended.

6. Transfer the mixture to the prepared pan. Place a large piece of parchment paper, wax paper, or plastic wrap (coated with nonstick cooking spray) atop the bar mixture and use it to spread and flatten the mixture evenly in the pan. Cover and refrigerate overnight until very firm.

7. Using the liner, lift the mixture from the pan and transfer to a cutting board. Uncover and cut into 9 bars. Store in the refrigerator or freezer.

Nutrients per bar: Calories 195, Fat 8.6 g, (Saturated 4.5 g), Cholesterol 11 mg, Sodium 99 mg, Carbs 18.9 g (Fiber 4.7 g, Sugars 8 g), Protein 9.4 g

BAR TIPS

—Consider adding up to 1/2 cup chopped dried fruit, 1/3 cup miniature semisweet chocolate chips, or 1/4 cup cacoa nibs to the quinoa mixture.

—Consider coating or drizzling the bars with any of the bar coatings on page 31.

—Coconut oil adds a subtle coconut flavor to these bars, but it also helps to hold them together. Hence, vegetable oil will not work in its place. The best all-natural alternative is unsalted butter.

—To boost the protein content of these bars even higher, replace the oats with an equal amount of quinoa flakes. You may also decrease the flaxseed meal to 1/4 cup and increase the total amount of protein powder to 3/4 cup.

—An equal amount of all-natural, sweetened vanilla whey protein powder may be used in place of the vegan protein powder. Increase the total amount of oats to 1 1/4 cups.

BAR KEEPING

Tightly wrap the bars individually in plastic wrap.

REFRIGERATOR: 1 week
FREEZER: 3 months in airtight container; thaw 1 hour

BAR VARIATIONS

LEMON-GINGER QUINOA PROTEIN BARS
Use honey as the sweetener. Add 2 teaspoons ground ginger along with the oats. Add 1 tablespoon finely grated lemon zest along with the honey.

WINTER SPICE QUINOA PROTEIN BARS
Use dark (cooking) molasses for the sweetener. Add 1 1/2 teaspoons ground cinnamon, 1 teaspoon ground ginger, 1/2 teaspoon ground cardamom, and 1/8 teaspoon ground cloves along with the oats.

QUINOA-CACAO PROTEIN BARS
Use an equal amount of chocolate vegan protein powder in place of the vanilla protein powder. Reduce the total amount of flaxseed meal to 1/4 cup and add 3 tablespoons unsweetened, natural cocoa powder along with the oats.

RAW
& ALMOST RAW
BARS

These bars are made with a minimal number of ingredients—all of which are raw or dehydrated rather than cooked. Preparation of the bars is a cinch given the lack of cooking: simply combine the ingredients and press into shape. Numerous variations of raw food diets exist, so you can decide whether to make these bars raw or "almost" raw. For example, if following a strictly raw diet, opt for all organic ingredients and use raw versions of honey, nut and seed butters, cocoa powder, and flake coconut.

GET UP & GOJI BARS

1 cup packed pitted, soft dates

1 cup warm water

1/3 cup natural, unsweetened raw nut or seed butter (e.g., peanut, cashew, or sunflower)

1/2 teaspoon ground cardamom

1 2/3 cups old-fashioned or quick-cooking rolled oats

2/3 cup dried goji berries, dried cherries, or dried cranberries, finely chopped

1/2 cup raw cashews, chopped

1/2 cup unsweetened flake or shredded coconut

1/3 cup chia seeds or poppy seeds

2 tablespoons flaxseed meal

Those who know and love me will tell you I am very frugal (except they would likely select a less flattering adjective). I prefer to say that I am careful with my spending, especially when it comes to food shopping. I tell you this because I am not the person at the health food store throwing every new superfood into my hand-basket with nary a thought of price; rather, I'm the woman making a beeline to the bulk goods and comparing the price per ounce on every item. So when I do recommend a particular superfood-splurge, it's because I think it's truly worth it. Case in point, goji berries. Goji berries are bright orange-red berries that come from a shrub that's native to China and they have a unique taste akin to dried cherries and cranberries. A lot of nutrition gets packed into a single berry, including powerful antioxidants, 18 different amino acids, and up to 21 trace minerals, including zinc, iron, copper, and calcium. **MAKES 16 BARS**

1. Line an 8-inch square baking pan with foil or parchment paper and grease the pan with coconut oil or vegetable oil.

2. Combine the dates and warm water in a small bowl. Let stand for 5 to 10 minutes until fruit is soft (time will vary according to the dryness of the dates). Drain and pat dry with paper towels.

3. Place the dates, nut or seed butter, and cardamom in a food processor and process until the mixture forms a thick paste; transfer to a large mixing bowl.

4. To the date mixture, add the oats, goji berries, cashews, coconut, chia seeds, and flaxseed meal; stir until well mixed (mixture will be very stiff).

5. Transfer the mixture to the prepared pan. Place a large piece of parchment paper, wax paper, or plastic wrap (lightly greased with coconut or vegetable oil) atop the bar mixture and use it to spread and flatten the mixture evenly in the pan; leave the paper or plastic wrap to cover. Refrigerate for at least 1 hour.

6. Using the liner, lift the mixture from the pan and transfer to a cutting board. Uncover and cut into 16 bars.

Nutrients per bar: Calories 178, Fat 9.1 g, (Saturated 2.9 g), Cholesterol 0 mg, Sodium 40 mg, Carbs 21.8 g (Fiber 4.6 g, Sugars 10.3 g), Protein 5.3 g

BAR TIPS

—Use raw, dehydrated coconut if following a strictly raw diet; if not, feel free to use regular unsweetened flake or shredded coconut and any variety—including roasted—of natural, unsweetened nut or seed butter.

—Cardamom adds an exotic flavor to these bars, but you can skip it if it's not already in your pantry. Consider adding an equal amount of ground ginger in its place.

BAR KEEPING

Tightly wrap the bars individually in plastic wrap.

ROOM TEMP: 2 days
REFRIGERATOR: 1 week
FREEZER: 3 months in airtight container; thaw 1 hour

BAR VARIATION

RAW MANGO MOJO BARS
Replace the goji berries with an equal amount of chopped, dried unsweetened mango and replace the cardamom with 3/4 teaspoon ground ginger. Add 2 teaspoons finely grated lime zest and 2 teaspoons fresh lime juice along with the dates.

LEMONY SPIRULINA BARS

1 1/3 cups packed dried figs or dried apricots

1 cup warm water

1 cup raw cashews

1 1/2 tablespoons spirulina powder

1/4 cup flaxseed meal

1 tablespoon finely grated lemon zest

2 tablespoons fresh lemon juice

Spirulina may sound like it's from outer space or from a creepy new line of Barbie dolls. In truth, it's not quite as scary. Simply stated, spirulina is a blue-green algae that thrives in brackish pond water and is profoundly high in nutrients. The World Health Organization, for example, has endorsed it as a vitamin- and protein-rich food supplement for undernourished people, and researchers indicate that the organism may help protect against a host of infectious diseases and even cancer. No need to troll the local backwater—it is readily available as a bright green powder at health food stores and can be added to smoothies and juices or into energy bars like this lemony version of my design. **MAKES 6 BARS**

1. Line a 9 by 5-inch loaf pan with plastic wrap and grease the pan with coconut oil or vegetable oil.

2. Combine the figs and warm water in a small bowl. Let stand for 5 to 10 minutes until fruit is soft (time will vary according to the dryness of the figs). Drain and pat dry with paper towels.

3. Meanwhile, place the cashews, spirulina powder, and flaxseed meal in a food processor and process until the cashews are very finely chopped (but not a paste). Add the drained figs, lemon zest, and lemon juice. Process, using on/off pulses, until the figs are finely chopped and blended and the mixture begins to stick together and clump on the sides of the bowl.

4. Transfer the mixture to the prepared pan. Place a large piece of parchment paper, wax paper, or plastic wrap (lightly greased with coconut or vegetable oil) atop the bar mixture and use it to spread and flatten the mixture evenly in the pan; leave the paper or plastic wrap to cover. Refrigerate for 30 minutes.

5. Using the liner, lift the mixture from the pan and transfer to a cutting board. Uncover and cut into 6 bars.

Nutrients per bar: Calories 254, Fat 12.9 g, (Saturated 2.4 g), Cholesterol 0 mg, Sodium 28 mg, Carbs 31 g (Fiber 4.3 g, Sugars 18.5 g), Protein 7.3 g

BAR TIPS

—I prefer these bars made with figs or apricots to emphasize the fresh flavor of the citrus and spirulina, but you can use any dried fruit you prefer or have on hand. Dates and golden raisins, for example, also make very tasty bars.

—Spirulina and citrus are made for each other, so experiment with equal amounts of zest and juice from other citrus fruits besides lemon. Think lime, orange, grapefruit, tangerine, or my new favorite, yuzu.

BAR KEEPING

Tightly wrap the bars individually in plastic wrap.

ROOM TEMP: 3 days
REFRIGERATOR: 1 week
FREEZER: 3 months in airtight container; thaw 1 hour

BAR VARIATIONS

GREEN APPLE BARS
Replace the figs with a combination of 3/4 cup packed pitted, soft dates and 3/4 cup dried apples. Omit the lemon zest and lemon juice and add 1 teaspoon vanilla extract and 1/2 teaspoon ground cinnamon along with the drained dried fruit.

GREEN COCONUT BARS
Replace the dried figs with an equal amount of packed, pitted, soft dates. Reduce the total amount of cashews to 3/4 cup and add 2/3 cup dried unsweetened flake or shredded coconut. Replace the lemon zest and lemon juice with equal amounts of lime zest and lime juice.

GREEN CHOCOLATE BARS
Replace the dried figs with an equal amount of packed, pitted, soft dates. Omit the lemon zest and lemon juice and reduce the total amount of cashews to 1 cup. Add 1/4 cup raw, unsweetened, natural cocoa powder.

CHOCOLATE HEMP
PROTEIN BARS

1 1/4 cups packed pitted, soft dates

1 cup warm water

1 cup hemp hearts (shelled hemp seeds)

1 cup unsweetened flake or shredded coconut

1/4 cup raw pepitas (green pumpkin seeds)

1/4 cup raw sesame seeds

1 cup raw, all-natural, sweetened chocolate vegan protein powder

1/3 cup old-fashioned or quick-cooking oats

1/3 cup virgin coconut oil, warmed until melted

1/4 cup raw, unsweetened, natural cocoa powder

1 teaspoon vanilla extract (omit, if strictly raw)

Prepare to meet your new obsession: hemp hearts. Hemp hearts are shelled hemp seeds and are among the most nutritious foods on the planet. No joke. Just one tablespoon of hemp hearts has a whopping 5 grams of protein and 5 grams of fiber. Additionally, they are very high in omega-3 essential fatty acids, and are an excellent source of iron, vitamin E, GLA (gamma-linolenic acid), and omega-6 fatty acids. But it's the flavor of these sesame-sized seeds—akin to raw walnuts, but without the bitterness—along with their ease of use and versatility that will win you over. No toasting or grinding required, just open a bag and start sprinkling away into smoothies, yogurt, baked goods, soups, stews...or these mega-healthy hemp protein bars. Rich and fudgy, you'll find it hard to believe that they are raw! **MAKES 16 BARS**

1. Line a 9-inch square baking pan with foil or parchment paper and grease the pan with coconut oil or vegetable oil.

2. Combine the dates and warm water in a small bowl. Let stand for 5 to 10 minutes until fruit is soft (time will vary according to the dryness of the dates). Drain and pat dry with paper towels.

3. Meanwhile, place the hemp hearts, coconut, pepitas, sesame seeds, protein powder, and oats in a food processor and process until coarsely chopped. Add the drained dates, oil, cocoa powder, and vanilla. Process, using on/off pulses, until the dates are finely chopped and blended and the mixture begins to stick together and clump on the sides of the bowl.

4. Transfer the mixture to the prepared pan. Place a large piece of parchment paper, wax paper, or plastic wrap (lightly greased with coconut or vegetable oil) atop the bar mixture and use it to spread and flatten the mixture evenly in the pan; leave the paper or plastic wrap to cover. Refrigerate for at least 2 hours.

5. Using the liner, lift the mixture from the pan and transfer to a cutting board. Uncover and cut into 16 bars.

Nutrients per bar: Calories 233, Fat 15.2 g, (Saturated 8.1 g), Cholesterol 4 mg, Sodium 33 mg, Carbs 15.9 g (Fiber 3.2 g, Sugars 9.9 g), Protein 10.9 g

BAR TIPS

—An equal amount of raw sunflower seeds or raw cashews may be used in place of the hemp seeds.

—An equal amount of raw, all-natural, sweetened vanilla vegan protein powder can be used in place of the chocolate protein powder; the flavor will be only marginally less chocolate-y.

—Coconut oil adds a subtle coconut flavor to these bars, but it also helps to hold them together. Hence, vegetable oil will not work in its place. You can, instead, substitute an equal amount of natural, unsweetened raw nut or seed butter or, if you have access to it, raw butter.

—If you are not following a strictly raw diet, there is no need to seek out raw cocoa powder, protein powder, or coconut; simply use readily available varieties.

—For optimal freshness, store the hemp seeds, and all other seeds and nuts, in an airtight container in the freezer.

BAR KEEPING

Tightly wrap the bars individually in plastic wrap.

ROOM TEMP: 2 days
REFRIGERATOR: 1 week
FREEZER: 3 months in airtight container; thaw 1 hour

BAR VARIATIONS

CASHEW-COCONUT PROTEIN BARS
Replace the hemp hearts, pepitas, and sesame seeds with 2 cups raw cashews. Omit the cocoa powder and use 3/4 cup raw, all-natural, sweetened vanilla vegan protein powder in place of the chocolate protein powder.

PALEO CHOCOLATE HEMP BARS
Omit the oats and protein powder. Increase the cocoa powder to 1/3 cup and increase the pepitas to 2/3 cup.

CHIA CHOCOLATE HEMP BARS
Replace the pepitas and sesame seeds with 1 cup chia seeds.

ROSE CHOCOLATE HEMP BARS
Prepare as directed, but add 1 teaspoon rose water and 3/4 teaspoon ground cardamom.

RAW BUCKWHEAT
GRANOLA BARS

3/4 cup raw buckwheat groats

3 cups water, divided

1 1/2 cups packed pitted, soft dates

3/4 cup raw seeds or nuts (e.g., hemp hearts, pepitas, almonds)

2 teaspoons vanilla extract (omit, if strictly raw)

1 teaspoon ground cinnamon

1/4 teaspoon fine sea salt

1/2 cup goji berries or dried cherries

My husband is the first person to let me know if I've gone off-track with my recipe experimentations, whether the results are overwrought, underwhelming, or just plain weird. Hence, his enthusiastic "thumbs up" for these bars should assure you that raw buckwheat groat bars are something you need to make ASAP. If you are nervous about soaking grains, don't be; it is very easy, and buckwheat groats are a great place to begin since they require less soaking time than other grains. Technically, buckwheat isn't a grain at all; rather, it is a distant relative of rhubarb. The groats are the hulled, crushed kernels of the buckwheat plant. It is a gluten-free grain, which makes these bars a perfect choice for anyone with celiac disease or any kind of gluten sensitivity. Consider this a beginning template for all kinds of fresh flavor variations—might I suggest my fresh ginger variation as a top contender?—and savor how energized these bars make you feel! MAKES 10 BARS

1. Line an 8-inch square baking pan with foil or parchment paper and grease the pan with coconut oil or vegetable oil.

2. Combine the buckwheat groats with 2 cups of the water in a large bowl. Loosely cover with a clean dish towel and let soak for 2 hours. Drain and rinse the groats in a strainer.

3. Place the groats in the same clean dish towel. Gather and twist the ends of the towel; squeeze out as much liquid as possible from the groats.

4. Warm the remaining 1 cup water and combine with the dates in a small bowl. Let stand for 5 to 10 minutes until fruit is soft (time will vary according to the dryness of the dates). Drain and pat dry with paper towels.

5. Meanwhile, place the seeds or nuts in a food processor and process until chopped (but not a paste). Add the drained dates, vanilla, cinnamon, and salt. Process, using on/off pulses, until the mixture is blended. Add the drained groats and goji berries; process, using on/off pulses, until the mixture is blended.

Nutrients per bar: Calories 161, Fat 4.2 g, (Saturated 0 g), Cholesterol 0 mg, Sodium 2 mg, Carbs 30.9 g (Fiber 4.3 g, Sugars 20 g), Protein 3.4 g

6. Transfer the mixture to the prepared pan. Place a large piece of parchment paper, wax paper, or plastic wrap (lightly greased with coconut or vegetable oil) atop the bar mixture and use it to spread and flatten the mixture evenly in the pan; leave the paper or plastic wrap to cover. Refrigerate for at least 4 hours or overnight.

7. Using the liner, lift the mixture from the pan and transfer to a cutting board. Uncover and cut into 10 bars. Store in the refrigerator or freezer.

BAR TIPS

—Be sure to get raw buckwheat groats— they look like extra-thick rolled oats—as opposed to toasted buckwheat (kasha) or buckwheat cereal; the latter two are not raw and, moreover, will lead to very different results.

—An equal amount of whole oat groats (not rolled oats) may be used in place of the buckwheat groats.

BAR KEEPING

Tightly wrap the bars individually in plastic wrap.

REFRIGERATOR: 1 week
FREEZER: 3 months in airtight container; thaw 1 hour

BAR VARIATIONS

RAW DOUBLE CACAO GRANOLA BARS
Reduce the total amount of seeds or nuts to 1/2 cup and add 1/3 cup raw, unsweetened, natural cocoa powder along with the seeds. Add 1/4 cup cacao nibs along with the drained groats.

FRESH GINGER BUCKWHEAT BARS
Omit the cinnamon and vanilla and add 1 tablespoon minced fresh ginger, 2 teaspoons finely grated lime zest, and 2 teaspoons fresh lime juice along with the drained groats.

MUST-HAVE-CHOCOLATE
RAW BARS

1 1/2 cups packed pitted, soft dates

1 cup warm water

1 cup raw cashews

1/3 cup old-fashioned or quick-cooking rolled oats

1/4 cup raw, all-natural, sweetened chocolate vegan protein powder

1/3 cup raw, unsweetened, natural cocoa powder

1 tablespoon virgin coconut oil, warmed until melted

1 teaspoon vanilla extract (omit, if strictly raw)

1/8 teaspoon fine sea salt

I don't want to be too dramatic, but if you don't find these fudgy, intensely chocolate-y raw brownies out of this world then we simply cannot be friends. They are just that good! And teeming with über-healthy ingredients! And a breeze to prepare! Is that too many exclamation points?! The cocoa made me do it.
MAKES 10 BARS

1. Line a 9 by 5-inch loaf pan with plastic wrap and grease the pan with coconut oil or vegetable oil.

2. Combine the dates and warm water in a small bowl. Let stand for 5 to 10 minutes until fruit is soft (time will vary according to the dryness of the dates). Drain and pat dry with paper towels.

3. Meanwhile, place the cashews and oats in a food processor and process until very finely chopped (but not a paste). Add the drained dates, protein powder, cocoa powder, oil, vanilla, and salt. Process, using on/off pulses, until the dates are finely chopped and blended and the mixture begins to stick together and clump on the sides of the bowl.

4. Transfer the mixture to the prepared pan. Place a piece of parchment paper, wax paper, or plastic wrap (lightly greased with coconut or vegetable oil) atop the bar mixture and use it to spread and flatten the mixture evenly in the pan; leave the paper or plastic wrap to cover. Refrigerate for 1 hour until firm.

5. Using the liner, lift the mixture from the pan and transfer to a cutting board. Uncover and cut into 10 bars.

Nutrients per bar: Calories 198, Fat 8.8 g, (Saturated 2.9 g), Cholesterol 0 mg, Sodium 85 mg, Carbs 26.1 g (Fiber 3.3 g, Sugars 15.6 g), Protein 7.8 g

BAR TIPS

—If you are not following a strictly raw diet, there is no need to seek out raw cocoa powder or raw protein powder; simply use readily available varieties.

—An equal amount of raisins, prunes, or chopped dried figs may be used in place of the dates.

—An equal amount of raw, all-natural, sweetened vanilla vegan protein powder can be used in place of the chocolate protein powder; the flavor will be only marginally less chocolate-y.

BAR KEEPING

Tightly wrap the bars individually in plastic wrap.

ROOM TEMP: 2 days
REFRIGERATOR: 1 week
FREEZER: 3 months in airtight container; thaw 1 hour

BAR VARIATIONS

RAW POWER BLONDIES
Omit the cocoa powder and replace the chocolate protein powder with 3/4 cup raw, all-natural, sweetened vanilla vegan protein powder.

RAW CHOCOLATE CRUNCH BARS
Add 1/4 cup cacao nibs to the food processor along with the drained dates.

RAW GIANDUIA BARS
Use an equal amount of raw hazelnuts in place of the cashews.

RAW CHUNKY CHERRY CHOCOLATE BARS
Reduce the total amount of dates to 3/4 cup and to them add 3/4 cup dried cherries. Use an equal amount of raw pecans in place of the cashews.

RAW MAYAN CHOCOLATE BARS
Use an equal amount of raw almonds in place of the cashews. Add 3/4 teaspoon ground cinnamon and 1/2 teaspoon chipotle chile powder along with the salt.

RAW PALEO CHOCOLATE BARS
Omit the oats and protein powder. Increase the total amount of cashews to 1 1/3 cups and increase the total amount of cocoa powder to 1/2 cup. Add 1/4 cup flaxseed meal.

STICKY SESAME BARS
WITH RAW CHOCOLATE DRIZZLE

2 cups raw nuts (e.g., cashews, peanuts, pistachios, pecans)

1 cup raw sesame seeds

1/2 cup chia seeds or poppy seeds

1/2 cup raw agave nectar or raw honey

1/3 cup natural, unsweetened raw nut or seed butter (e.g., tahini, sunflower, or peanut)

2 tablespoons virgin coconut oil, warmed until melted

1 teaspoons vanilla extract (omit, if strictly raw)

1/4 teaspoon fine sea salt

RAW CHOCOLATE DRIZZLE

2 tablespoons virgin coconut oil, warmed until melted

2 tablespoons raw agave nectar or raw honey

2 tablespoons raw, unsweetened, natural cocoa powder (not Dutch process)

I'll eat just about anything with "sticky" in the title, which prompted me to create a sticky energy bar my raw foodie friends and I can savor together. I've cast sesame seeds in a lead role here because I'm tired of seeing one of my favorite ingredients marginalized atop hamburger buns and everything bagels—they have a terrific earthy-nutty flavor and a delicate crunch that goes well with so many dishes. Moreover, their nutritional profile will leave you star-struck. Sesame seeds are a very good source of manganese and copper and a good source of protein, calcium, magnesium, iron, phosphorus, vitamin B1, zinc, and dietary fiber. Further, they contain two special types of fiber, sesamin and sesamolin, which are members of the lignans group and can lower "bad" cholesterol and help prevent high blood pressure. And did I mention chocolate? Namely, raw chocolate drizzle? Sesame seeds plus raw chocolate drizzle equals crazy good. **MAKES 20 BARS**

1. Line an 8-inch square baking pan with foil or parchment paper and grease the pan with coconut oil or vegetable oil.

2. Place the nuts, sesame seeds, and chia seeds in a food processor and process until finely chopped. Add the agave nectar, nut or seed butter, oil, vanilla, and salt. Process, using on/off pulses, until the mixture is blended and begins to stick together and clump on the sides of the bowl.

3. Transfer the mixture to the prepared pan. Place a large piece of parchment paper, wax paper, or plastic wrap (lightly greased with coconut or vegetable oil) atop the bar mixture and use it to spread and flatten the mixture evenly in the pan; leave the paper or plastic wrap to cover. Place the mixture in the freezer for 30 minutes.

4. To prepare the chocolate drizzle: Mix the oil, agave nectar, and cocoa powder in a small bowl until blended. Remove the bar mixture from the freezer, uncover, and decoratively drizzle or spread with the chocolate mixture. Refrigerate for at least 4 hours or place in the freezer for 1 hour until the mixture is firm.

5. Using the liner, lift the mixture from the pan and transfer to a cutting board. Cut into 20 bars. Store in the refrigerator or freezer.

Nutrients per bar: Calories 201, Fat 15 g, (Saturated 3.8 g), Cholesterol 0 mg, Sodium 33 mg, Carbs 14.8 g (Fiber 4.5 g, Sugars 8.7 g), Protein 5.9 g

BAR TIPS

—Coconut oil helps to hold these bars together; vegetable oil will not work in its place. You can, instead, add an additional 2 tablespoons natural, unsweetened raw nut or seed butter or, if you have access to it, raw butter.

—If you are not following a raw diet, you can drizzle the bars with the Chocolate Bar Coating (see page 31).

BAR KEEPING

Tightly wrap the bars individually in plastic wrap.

REFRIGERATOR: 1 week
FREEZER: 3 months in airtight container; thaw 1 hour

BAR VARIATIONS

RAW HONEY BUN BARS

Use raw cashews as the nuts and raw honey as the sweetener. Replace the cocoa powder with an equal amount of raw, all-natural, sweetened vanilla vegan protein powder.

RAW STICKY ALMOND FUDGE BARS

Use 3 cups raw almonds for the nuts and omit the sesame seeds. Reduce the chia seeds to 1/4 cup and add 1/3 cup raw, unsweetened cocoa powder along with the agave nectar. Use raw almond butter for the nut butter.

INGREDIENT SOURCES

AMAZON
www.amazon.com
One-stop shop for every ingredient needed for making the bars in this collection, including raw ingredients (e.g., raw honey, raw agave, raw cocoa powder), protein powders (whey, vegan, and raw), nuts, green tea powder (matcha), dried fruits, and more. Many options for buying items in bulk.

ARTISANA ORGANIC FOODS
www.artisanafoods.com
Producer of raw, organic nut and seed butters as well as organic, raw, extra-virgin coconut oil.

BOB'S RED MILL
www.bobsredmill.com
A top-notch producer of whole grains, such as quinoa, oats, and wheat germ, as well as flaxseed meal, nuts, seeds, dried fruits, cacao nibs, hulled hemp seeds (hemp hearts), and unsweetened coconut. Many of the products are available in gluten-free or organic varieties.

EDEN FOODS
www.edenfoods.com
Producer of alternative grain flakes, including kamut, spelt, rye, and rice flakes, all of which can be used as a partial or entire substitution for rolled oats. Also an excellent source for other high-quality, organic ingredients including spices, expeller-pressed cooking oils, dried fruit, quinoa, and unseasoned beans packaged in BPA-free cans.

ENERGY FIRST
www.energyfirst.com
Producer of all-natural, highest-grade whey protein made from a cold-processing method. The whey is derived from farm-raised, pasture-grazed, grass-fed cows that are not treated with the synthetic bovine growth hormone rBGH. The powders are free of sugar, gluten, artificial flavors, and artificial colors; they are sweetened using all-natural stevia.

FLORIDA CRYSTALS
www.floridacrystals.com
Producer of a broad spectrum of minimally processed natural cane sugars, all of which are free of preservatives and artificial ingredients.

GARDEN OF LIFE
www.gardenoflife.com
Producers of raw, vegan protein powders made from high-quality plant sources, all of which are allergen-free, soy-free, non-GMO, naturally-flavored, and naturally sweetened with stevia.

JAY ROBB
www.jayrobb.com
Producer of all-natural, highest-grade whey protein made from a cold-processing method. The whey is derived from farm-raised, pasture-grazed, grass-fed cows that are not treated with the synthetic bovine growth hormone rBGH. The powders are free of sugar, gluten, artificial flavors, and artificial colors; they are sweetened using all-natural stevia.

MARANATHA FOODS
www.maranathafoods.com
Producer of natural nut and seed butters, including many organic and raw options.

NAVITA'S NATURALS
www.navitasnaturals.com
Producers of certified organic, minimally processed superfoods such as chia seeds, hemp hearts, cacao nibs, flaxseed meal, and goji berries.

NUTS.COM

www.nuts.com

One-stop online shop for bulk foods—including many raw and organic options—such as nuts, seeds (e.g., hemp, chia, pepita), dried fruits, organic natural cane sugars, organic unsweetened nut butters, cacao nibs, coconut, grains, quinoa flakes, barley flakes, spirulina, and so much more.

PENZEYS SPICES

www.penzeys.com

A shop with an unmatched variety of spices, extracts, and sea salts, all at excellent prices.

THE RAW FOOD WORLD

www.therawfoodworld.com

One-stop shopping for raw ingredients, including raw nut and seed butters, raw cocoa powder, raw protein powders, raw coconut flakes, and more.

SPECTRUM ORGANICS

www.spectrumorganics.com

Producer of expeller-pressed cooking oils (many of which are organic), coconut oil, and cooking sprays made without chlorofluorocarbons.

SUNSPIRE

www.sunspire.com

Producer of all-natural, grain-sweetened, high-quality chocolate chips (including semisweet, bittersweet, miniature, and white chocolate chips), carob chips, and baking chocolate. Also has an extensive selection of dairy-free (vegan) and gluten-free options.

SUNWARRIOR

www.sunwarrior.com

Producers of raw, vegan protein powders made from high quality plant sources, all of which are allergen-free, soy-free, non-GMO, naturally flavored, and naturally sweetened with stevia. Powders are available in gluten-free varieties.

SWEET LEAF

www.sweetleaf.com

Producer of an extensive assortment of 100% stevia products, all of which are derived from a chemical-free, alcohol-free, purified water extraction method.

WHOLESOME SWEETENERS

www.wholesomesweeteners.com

Producer of agave nectar, honey, and sugars made without bleaching agents or bone char. Also a primary source for organic, light corn syrup.

VITACOST

www.vitacost.com

A one-stop shop for almost every ingredient you need for making the power bars in this collection—all at discount prices—including protein powders (whey, vegan, raw), spirulina, crisp brown rice cereal, stevia, natural nut and seed butters, regular and gluten-free rolled oats, quinoa, alternative grain flakes (e.g., quinoa flakes and rye flakes), organic spices, organic fruit nectars, natural sweeteners, and so much more.

INDEX

C